Andrew Catterall • Lynn Henfield • Christine Horbury

CW01597505

ESSENTIALS

AQA

GCSE Additional Science

Revision Guide

Contents

Contents

Revised

Chemistry Unit 2

Physics Unit 2

The numbers in brackets correspond to the reference numbers on the AQA GCSE Additional Science specification.

How to Use This Guide

This revision guide has been written and developed to help you get the most out of your revision.

This guide covers both Foundation and Higher Tier content.

HT Content that will only be tested on the Higher Tier papers appears in a pale yellow coloured box labelled with the HT symbol.

- The **coloured page headers** clearly identify the separate units, so that you can revise for each exam separately: Biology is red, Chemistry is purple, and Physics is blue.
- The exam will include questions on **How Science Works**, so make sure you work through the How Science Works section in green at the front of this guide before each exam.
- There are two **summary pages** at the end of each unit, which outline all the key points. These are great for a final recap before your exam.
- There are **practice questions** at the end of each unit so you can test yourself on what you've just learned. (The answers are given on pages 90–91 so you can mark your own answers.)
- You'll find **key words** in a yellow box on each 2-page spread. They are also highlighted in colour within the text; higher tier key words are highlighted in a different colour. Make sure you know and understand all these words before moving on!
- There's a **glossary** at the back of the book. It contains all the key words from throughout the book so you can check any definitions you're unsure of.
- The **tick boxes** on the contents page let you track your revision progress: simply put a tick in the box next to each topic when you're confident that you know it.
- Don't just read the guide, **learn actively**! Constantly test yourself without looking at the text.

Good luck with your exam!

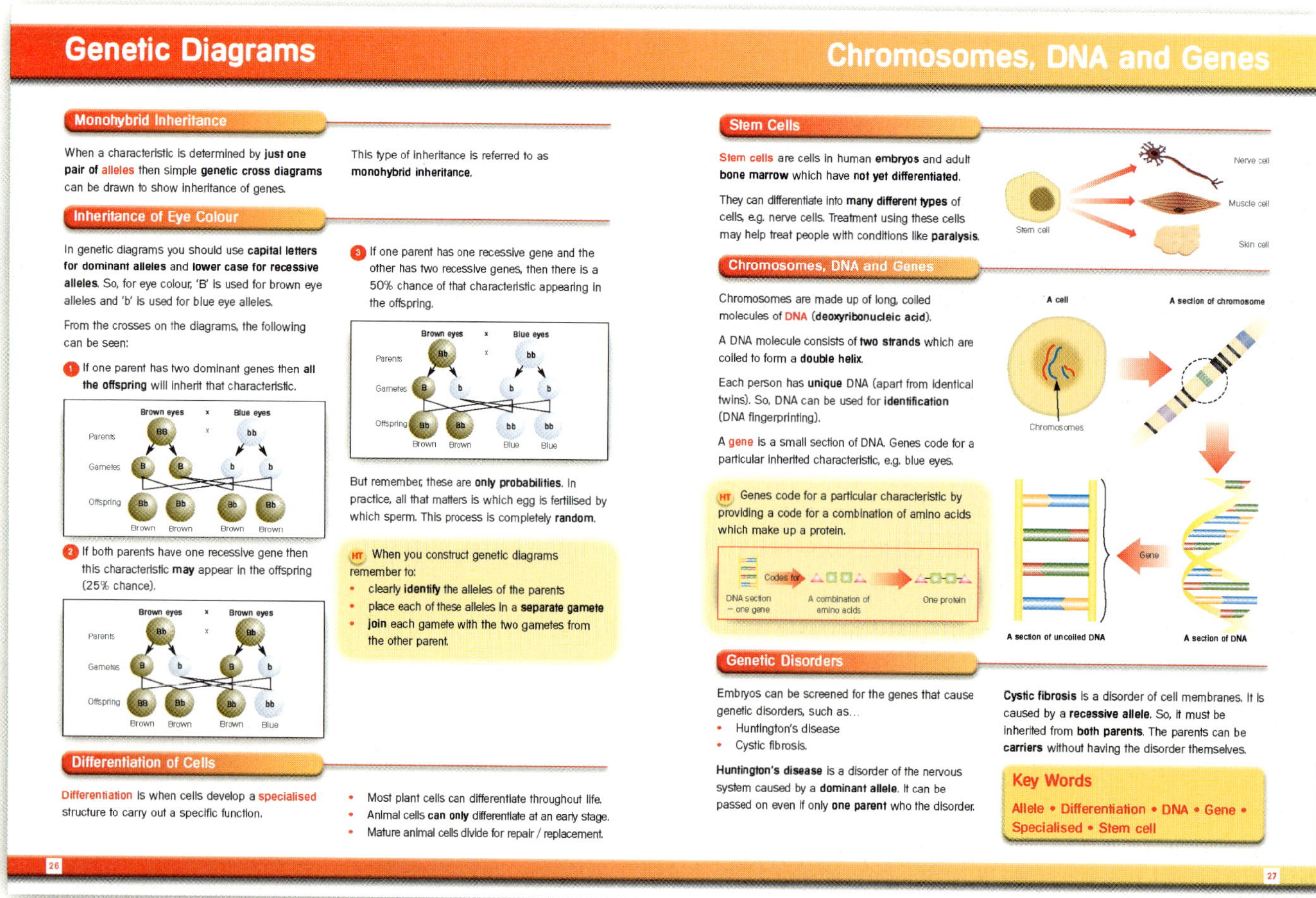

How Science Works – Explanation

The AQA GCSE Science specifications incorporate:

1. **Science Content** – all the scientific explanations and evidence that you need to know for the exam. (It is covered on pages 12–85 of this revision guide.)
2. **How Science Works** – a set of key concepts, relevant to all areas of science. It covers...
   - the relationship between scientific evidence, and scientific explanations and theories
   - how scientific evidence is collected
   - how reliable and valid scientific evidence is
   - the role of science in society
   - the impact science has on our lives
   - how decisions are made about the ways science and technology are used in different situations, and the factors affecting these decisions.

Your teacher(s) will have taught these two types of content together in your science lessons. Likewise, the questions on your exam papers will probably combine elements from both types of content. So, to answer the questions, you'll need to recall the relevant scientific facts *and* apply your knowledge of how science works.

The key concepts of How Science Works are summarised in this section of the revision guide (pages 6–11).

You should be familiar with all of these concepts. If there is anything you are unsure about, ask your teacher to explain it to you.

How Science Works is designed to help you learn about and understand the practical side of science. It aims to help you develop your skills when it comes to...

- evaluating information
- developing arguments
- drawing conclusions.

N.B. Practical tips on how to evaluate information are included on page 11.

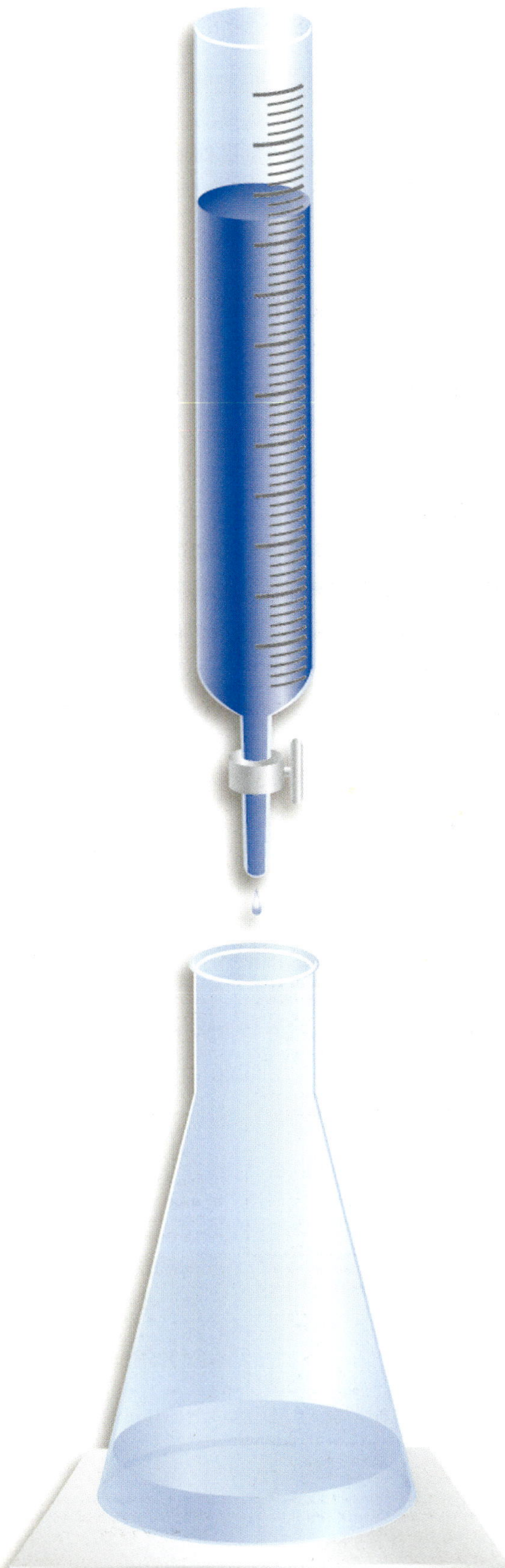

How Science Works

What is the Purpose of Science?

Science attempts to explain the world we live in.

Scientists carry out investigations and collect evidence in order to...

- **explain phenomena** (i.e. how and why things happen)
- **solve problems.**

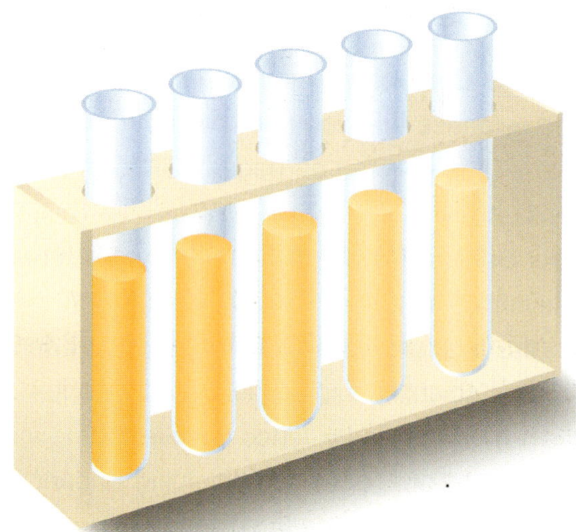

Scientific knowledge and understanding can lead to the **development of new technologies** (e.g. in medicine and industry), which have a huge impact on...

- society
- the environment.

What is the Purpose of Evidence?

Scientific evidence provides **facts** which answer a specific question and either **support** or **disprove** an idea / theory.

Evidence is often based on data that has been collected through...

- **observations**
- **measurements.**

To allow scientists to reach conclusions, evidence must be...

- **reliable** – it must be trustworthy
- **valid** – it must be reliable and answer the question.

N.B. If data isn't reliable, it can't be valid.

To ensure scientific evidence is reliable and valid, scientists use ideas and practices relating to...

1. observations
2. investigations
3. measurements
4. data presentation
5. conclusions.

These five key ideas are covered in more detail on the following pages.

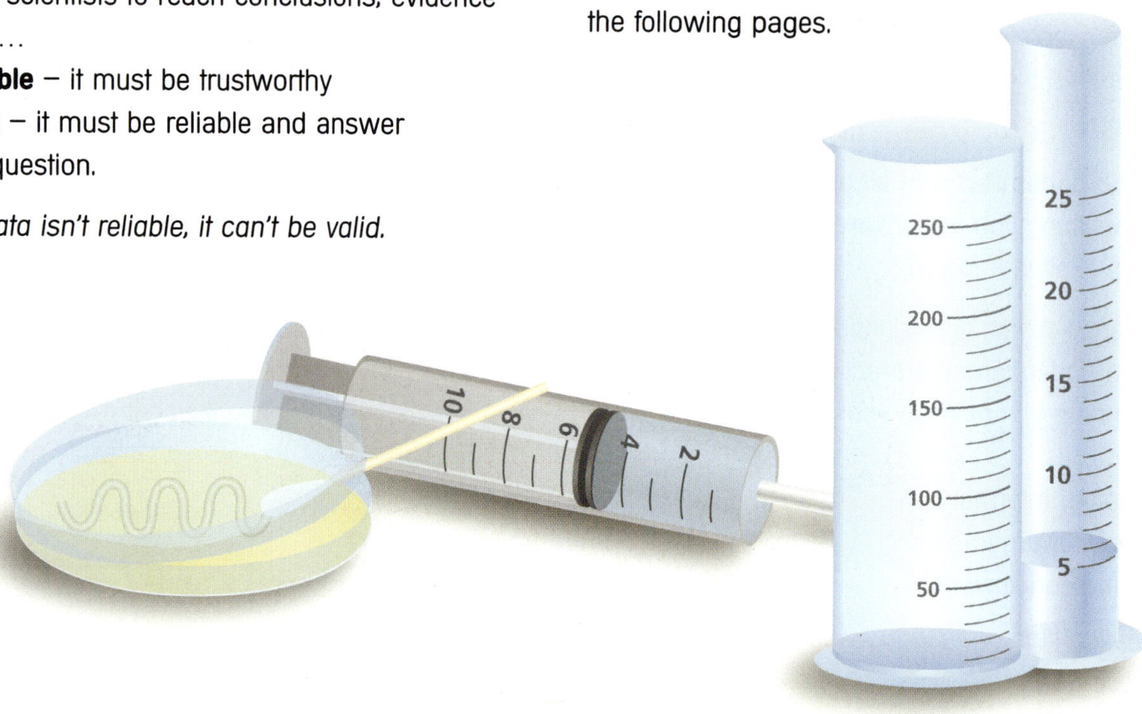

Observations

Most scientific investigations begin with an **observation**. A scientist observes an event / phenomenon and decides to find out more about how and why it happens.

The first step is to develop a **hypothesis** to suggest an explanation for the phenomenon. Hypotheses normally suggest a relationship between two or more **variables** (factors that change). Hypotheses are based on...

- careful observations
- existing scientific knowledge
- a bit of creative thinking.

The hypothesis is used to make a **prediction**, which can be tested through scientific investigation. The data collected from the investigation will...

- support the hypothesis **or**
- show it to be untrue **or**
- lead to the development of a new hypothesis.

If new observations or data don't match existing explanations or theories, they must be checked for reliability and validity.

Sometimes, if the new observations and data are valid, existing theories and explanations have to be revised or amended, and so scientific knowledge grows and develops.

Example

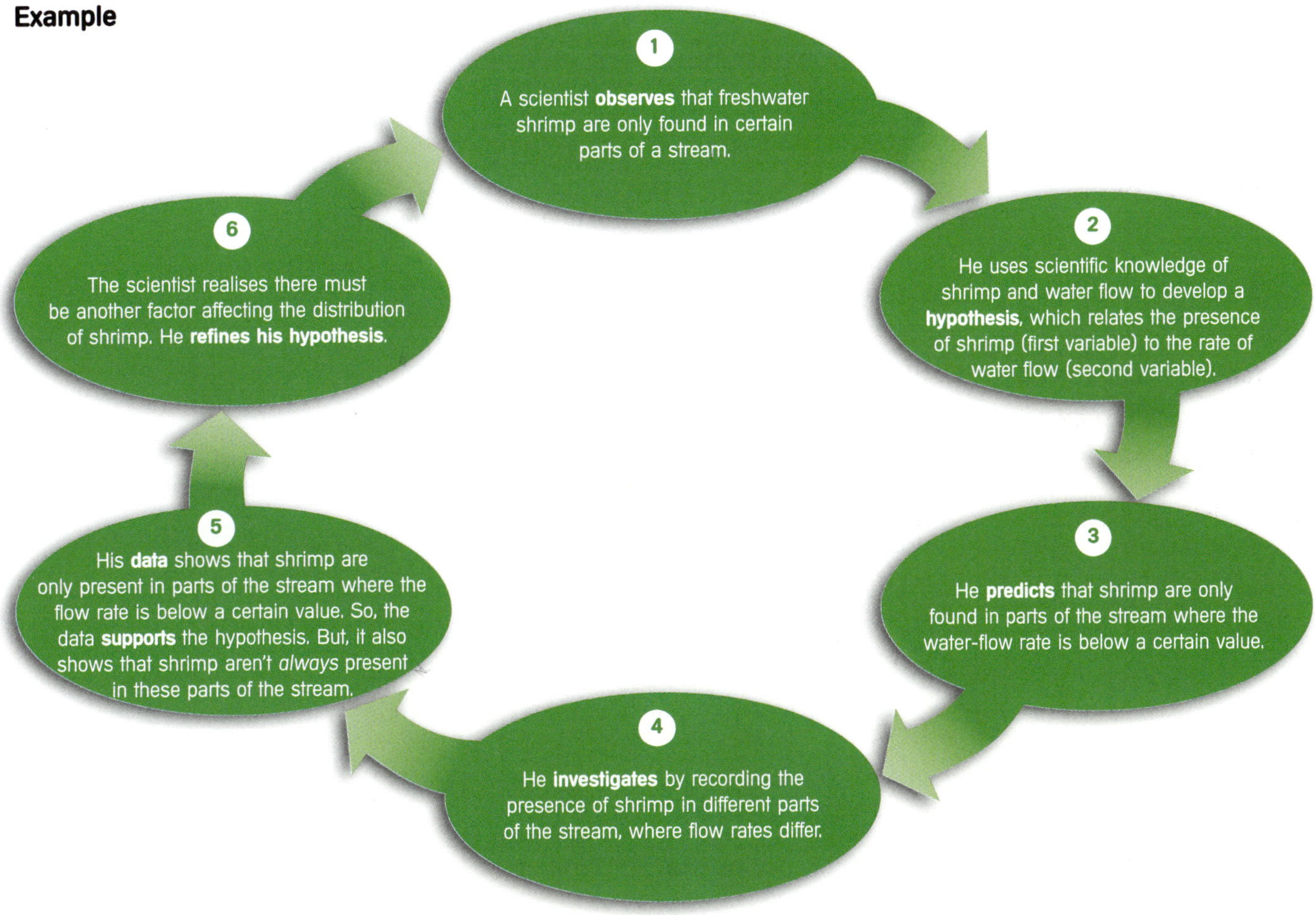

Investigations

An **investigation** involves collecting data to find out whether there is a relationship between two **variables**. A variable is a factor that can take different values.

In an investigation there are two variables:

1. **Independent variable** – can be adjusted (changed) by the person carrying out the investigation.
2. **Dependent variable** – measured each time a change is made to the independent variable, to see if it also changes.

Variables can have different types of values:

- **Continuous variables** – take numerical values. These are usually measurements, e.g. temperature.
- **Discrete variables** – only take whole-number values. These are usually quantities, e.g. the number of shrimp in a stream.
- **Ordered variables** – have relative values, e.g. 'small', 'medium' or 'large'.
- **Categoric variables** – have a limited number of specific values, e.g. different breeds of dog.

N.B. Numerical values tend to be more informative than ordered and categoric variables.

An investigation tries to find out whether an **observed** link between two variables is...

- **causal** – a change in one variable causes a change in the other
- **due to association** – the changes in the two variables are linked by a third variable
- **due to chance** – the change in the two variables is unrelated; it is coincidental.

Fair Tests

In a **fair test**, the only factor that can affect the dependent variable is the independent variable. Other **outside variables** that could influence the results are kept the same or eliminated.

It's a lot easier to carry out a fair test in the lab than in the field, where conditions can't always be controlled. The impact of an outside variable, like the weather, has to be reduced by ensuring all measurements are affected by it in the same way.

Accuracy and Precision

How accurate the data collected needs to be depends on what the investigation is trying to find out. For example, measures of alcohol in the blood must be accurate to determine whether a person is legally fit to drive.

The data collected must be **precise** enough to form a **valid conclusion**: it should provide clear evidence for or against the hypothesis.

To ensure data is as accurate as possible, you can...

- calculate the **mean** (average) of a set of repeated measurements to get a **best estimate** of the true value
- increase the number of measurements taken to improve the **accuracy** and the **reliability** of the mean.

Measurements

Apart from outside variables, there are a number of factors that can affect the reliability and validity of measurements:

- **Accuracy of instruments** – depends on how accurately the instrument has been calibrated. (Expensive equipment is usually more accurately calibrated.)
- **Sensitivity of instruments** – determined by the smallest change in value that the instrument can detect. For example, bathroom scales aren't sensitive enough to detect the changes in a baby's weight, but the scales used by a midwife are.
- **Human error** – can occur if you lose concentration. Systematic (repeated) errors can occur if the instrument hasn't been calibrated properly or is misused.

You need to examine any **anomalous** (irregular) values to try to determine why they appear. If they have been caused by an equipment failure or human error, it is common practice to discount them from any calculations.

Presenting Data

Data is often presented in a **chart** or **graph** because it makes...

- the patterns more evident
- it easier to see the relationship between two variables.

The relationship between variables can be...

- **linear** (positive or negative)
- **or directly proportional**.

If you present data clearly, it is easier to identify any anomalous values. The type of chart or graph you use to present data depends on the type of variable involved:

1. **Tables** organise data (but patterns and anomalies aren't always obvious).
2. **Bar charts** display data when the independent variable is categoric or discrete and the dependent variable is continuous.
3. **Line graphs** display data when both variables are continuous.
4. **Scattergrams** (scatter diagrams) show the underlying relationship between two variables. This can be made clearer if you include a **line of best fit**.

1

Height (cm)	127	165	149	147	155	161	154	138	145
Shoe Size	5	8	5	6	5	5	6	4	5

2

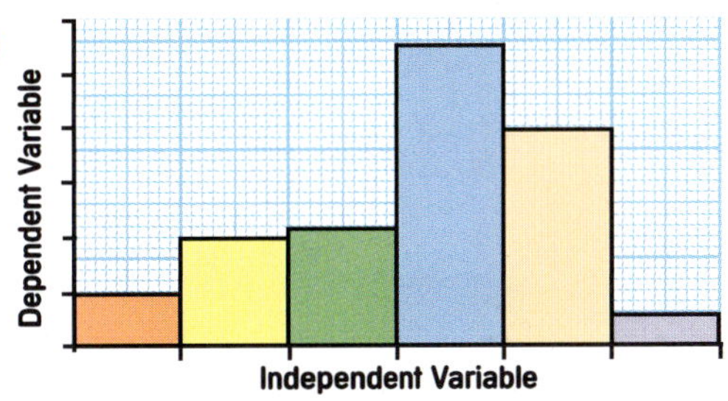

3

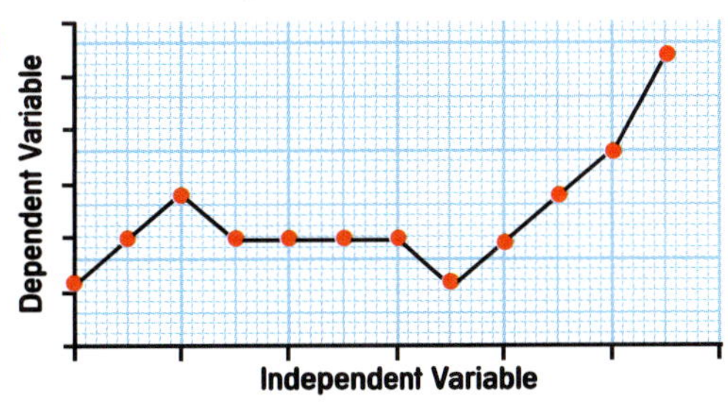

4

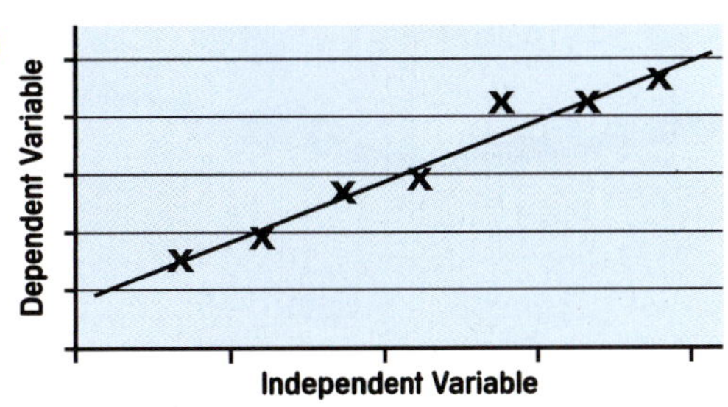

Conclusions

Conclusions **should**...

- describe the patterns and relationships between variables
- take all the data into account
- make direct reference to the original hypothesis / prediction.

Conclusions **shouldn't**...

- be influenced by anything other than the data collected
- disregard any data (except anomalous values)
- include any speculation.

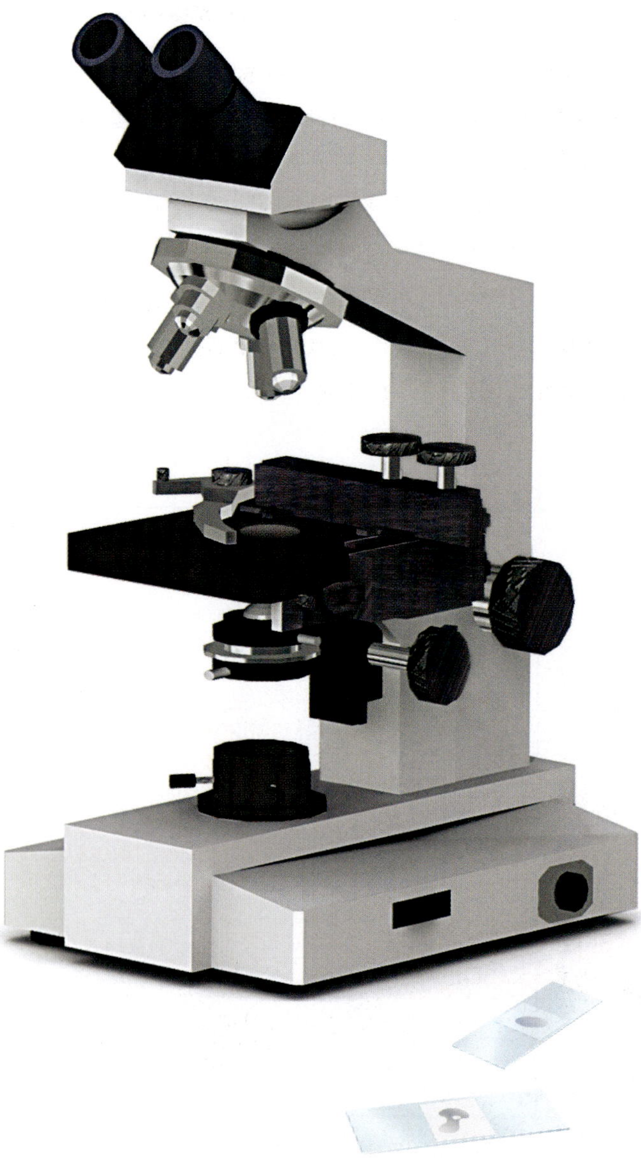

Evaluation

An **evaluation** looks at the whole investigation. It should consider...

- the original purpose of the investigation
- the appropriateness of the methods and techniques used
- the reliability and validity of the data
- the validity of the conclusions.

The **reliability** of an investigation can be increased by...

- looking at relevant data from secondary sources
- using an alternative method to check results
- ensuring that the results can be reproduced by others.

Science and Society

Scientific understanding can lead to technological developments. These developments can be exploited by different groups of people for different reasons. For example, the successful development of a new drug...

- benefits the drugs company financially
- improves the quality of life for patients.

Scientific developments can raise certain **issues**. An issue is an important question that is in dispute and needs to be settled. The resolution of an issue may not be based on scientific evidence alone.

There are several different **issues** which can arise:

- **Social** – the impact on the human population of a community, city, country, or the world.
- **Economic** – money and related factors like employment and the distribution of resources.
- **Environmental** – the impact on the planet, its natural ecosystems and resources.
- **Ethical** – what is morally right and wrong; requires a valued judgement to be made about what is acceptable.

N.B. There is often an overlap between social and economic issues.

Evaluating Information

It is important to be able to evaluate information relating to social-scientific issues, both for the exam and to help you make informed decisions in life.

When evaluating information...

- make a list of **pluses**
- make a list of **minuses**
- consider how each point might **impact on society**.

N.B. Remember, ***PMI*** *–* ***p****luses,* ***m****inuses,* ***i****mpact on society.*

You also need to consider whether the source of information is reliable and credible. Some important factors to consider are...

- **opinions**
- **bias**
- **weight of evidence**.

Opinions are personal viewpoints. Opinions backed up by valid and reliable evidence carry far more weight than those based on non-scientific ideas.

Information is **biased** if it favours one particular viewpoint without providing a balanced account. Biased information might include incomplete evidence or try to influence how you interpret the evidence.

Scientific evidence can be given **undue weight** or dismissed too lightly due to...

- political significance
- status (academic or professional status, experience, authority and reputation).

Limitations of Science

Although science can help us in lots of ways, it can't supply all the answers. We are still finding out about things and developing our scientific knowledge.

There are some questions that science can't answer. These tend to be questions relating to...

- ethical issues
- situations where it isn't possible to collect reliable and valid scientific evidence.

Science can often tell us if something **can** be done, and **how** it should be done, but it can't tell us whether it **should** be done.

Cells

Cells

All **living things** are made up of **cells**. The **structures** of different types of cells are related to their **functions**.

Cells may be **specialised** in order to carry out a particular job, as the table shows:

Chemical reactions inside cells are controlled by **enzymes**.

Enzymes are found in **cytoplasm** and **mitochondria**.

Root hair cells	Ovum (egg cell)	Xylem	White blood cells	Sperm cells	Palisade cells	Red blood cells	Nerve cells
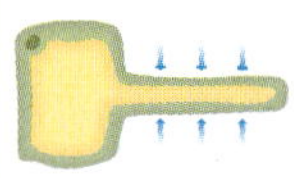		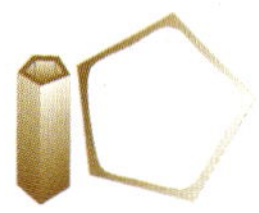	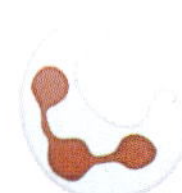	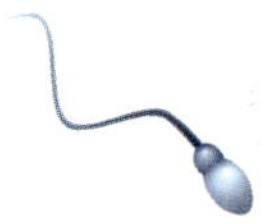			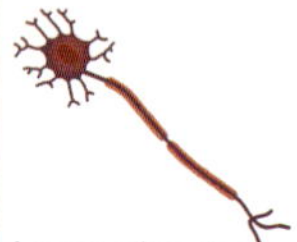
Tiny hair-like structures which increase surface area of the cell.	Large cell which can carry massive food reserves for the developing embryo.	Long, thin, hollow cells used to transport water through the stem and root.	Can change shape in order to engulf and destroy invading microorganisms.	Has a tail which allows it to move.	Packed with chloroplasts for photosynthesis.	No nucleus, so packed full of haemoglobin.	Long, slender axons which can carry nerve impulses.

Animal Cells

Human cells, most animal cells, and plant cells have the following parts:

- **Nucleus** – controls the activities of the cell.
- **Cytoplasm** – where most chemical reactions take place.
- A **cell membrane** – controls the passage of substances in and out of the cell.
- **Mitochondria** – where most energy is released in **respiration**.
- **Ribosomes** – where protein synthesis occurs.

A Human Cheek Cell

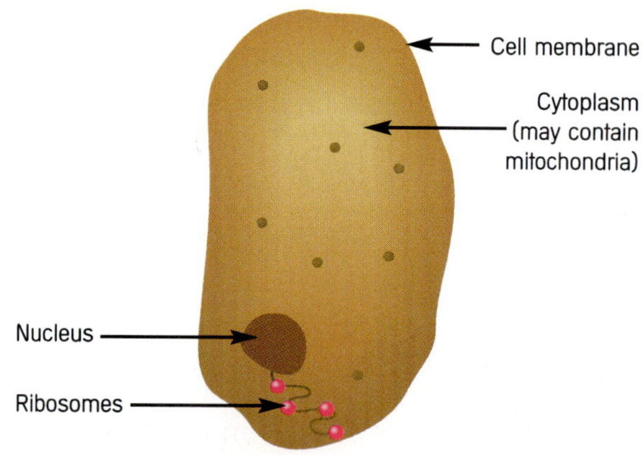

Plant Cells

Plant cells also have the following parts:

- A **cell wall** – used to strengthen the cell.
- **Chloroplasts** – absorb light energy to make food.
- A **permanent vacuole** – filled with cell sap.

A Palisade Cell from a Leaf

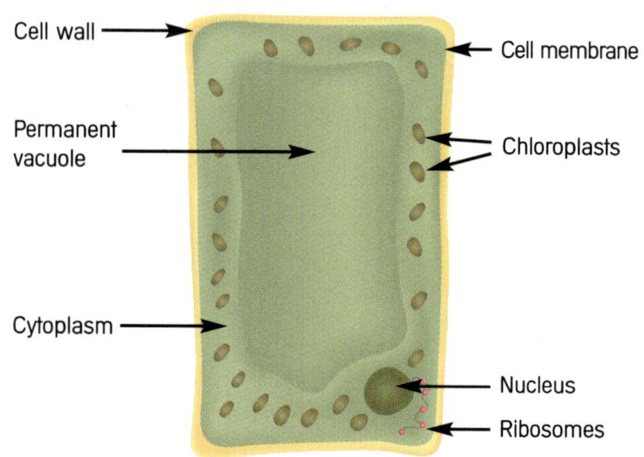

Key Words

Cell • Chloroplast • Cytoplasm • Diffusion • Enzyme • Mitochondria • Nucleus • Osmosis • Respiration • Ribosomes • Specialised • Vacuole

The Movement of Substances

Cells have to constantly...

- **replace** substances which are used up, e.g. food and oxygen
- **remove** other substances, e.g. carbon dioxide and waste products.

These substances can pass into and out of cells by...

- **diffusion**
- **osmosis**.

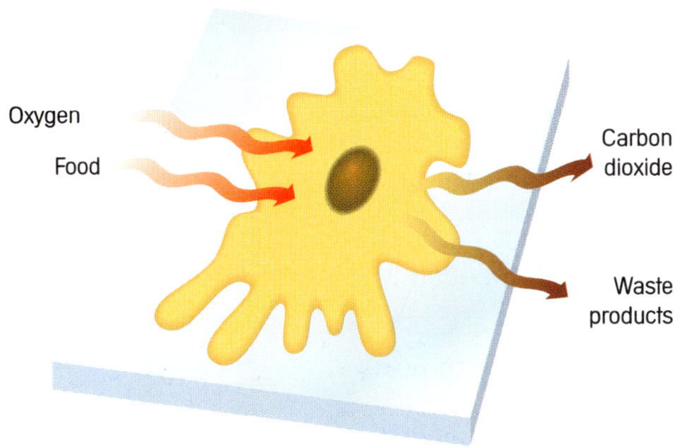

Diffusion

Diffusion is the spreading of the **particles of a gas**, or any substance in solution, which results in a **net movement** from a region where they are at a **higher concentration**, to a region where they are at a **lower concentration**.

Oxygen required for **respiration** passes through cell membranes by diffusion. The **greater the difference** in concentration, the **faster the rate** of diffusion.

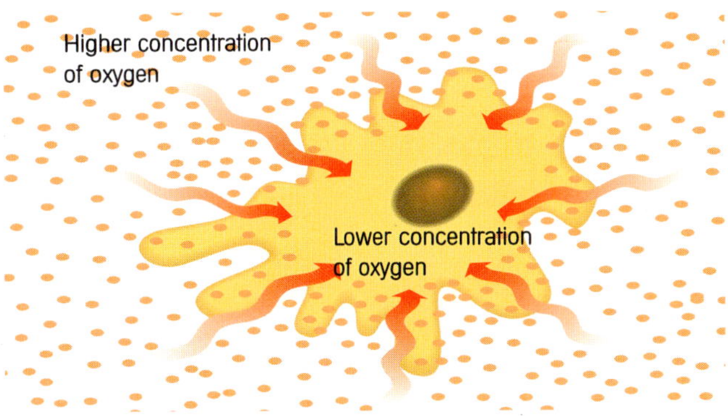

Osmosis

Osmosis is the **movement of water** from a **dilute solution** to a **more concentrated solution** through a partially permeable membrane.

The membrane allows the passage of water molecules, but not solute molecules because they are too large.

Osmosis will gradually **dilute** the more concentrated solution. For example, at root hair cells water moves from the soil into the cell by osmosis, along a concentration gradient.

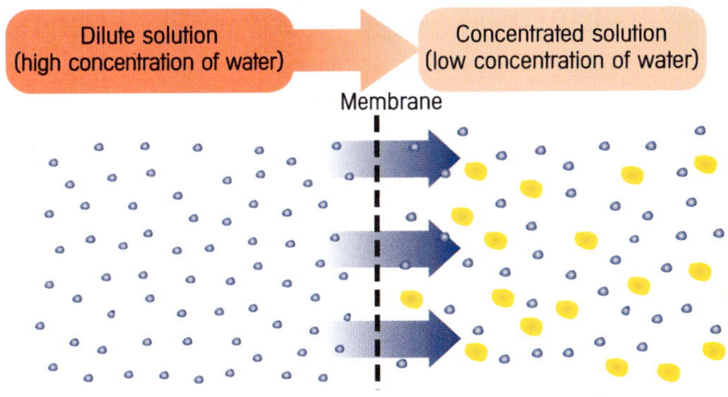

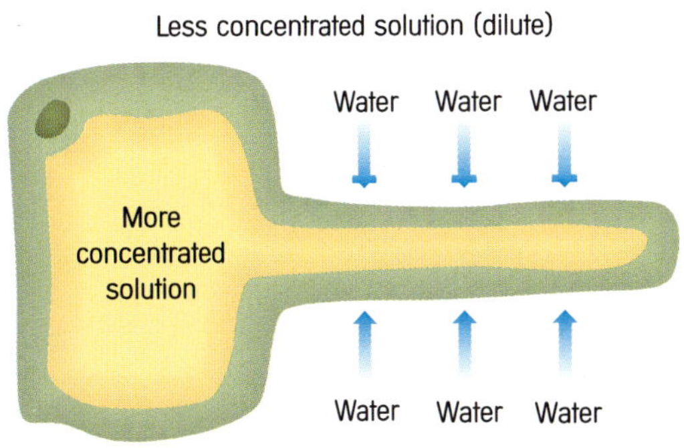

Photosynthesis

Plant Mineral Requirements

For healthy growth, plants need **mineral ions** which they absorb from the soil through their roots. The necessary mineral ions include...

- **nitrates**
- **magnesium**.

Nitrates are needed to make amino acids which are used to make **proteins**. A shortage of nitrates leads to stunted growth.

Magnesium is needed for **chlorophyll production**. A shortage leads to yellow leaves.

Photosynthesis

Green plants don't absorb food from the soil. They make their own using sunlight. This process is called **photosynthesis**.

Photosynthesis occurs in the cells of **green plants** which are exposed to light.

During photosynthesis, light energy is absorbed by green **chlorophyll** which is found in chloroplasts in some plant cells.

The **light energy** is used to convert **carbon dioxide** and **water** into **sugar** (glucose).

Four things are needed for photosynthesis:

- **light** from the Sun
- **carbon dioxide** from the air
- **water** from the soil
- **chlorophyll** in the leaves.

Two things are produced:

- **sugar** (glucose)
- **oxygen** – released into the atmosphere as a by-product.

The word equation for photosynthesis is...

$$\text{Carbon dioxide} + \text{Water} \xrightarrow[\text{chlorophyll}]{\text{light}} \text{Glucose} + \text{Oxygen}$$

The glucose produced in photosynthesis can be...

- used by the plant to provide **energy** for **respiration**
- converted into **insoluble starch** which is stored in the stem, leaves or roots.

Factors Affecting Photosynthesis

Factors Affecting Photosynthesis

There are several factors that may at any time **limit the rate** of photosynthesis:

- **temperature**
- **carbon dioxide** (CO_2) concentration
- **light intensity**.

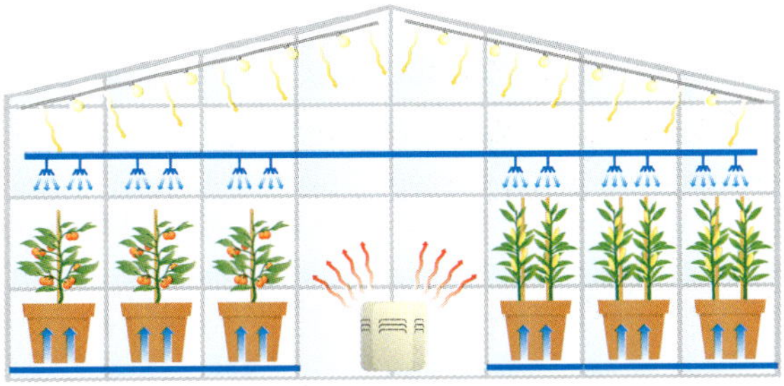

Temperature

1. As the temperature increases, so does the rate of photosynthesis. Temperature is limiting the rate of photosynthesis.
2. As the temperature approaches 45°C, the rate of photosynthesis drops to zero. The enzymes controlling photosynthesis have been destroyed.

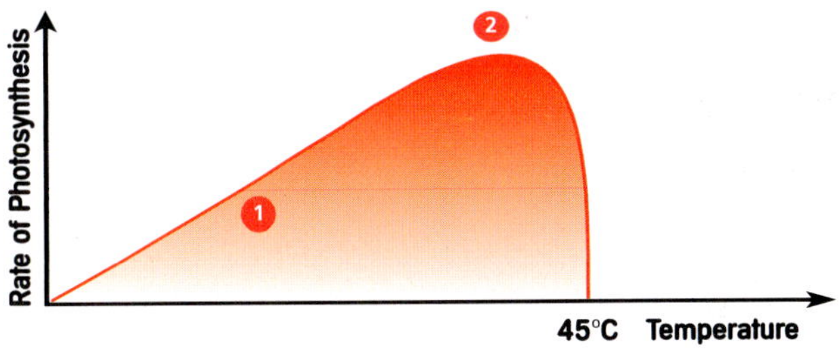

Carbon Dioxide Concentration

1. As the rate of carbon dioxide concentration increases, so does the rate of photosynthesis. CO_2 is limiting the rate of photosynthesis.
2. After reaching a certain point, an increase in carbon dioxide has no further effect. Carbon dioxide is no longer the limiting factor – it must be either light or temperature.

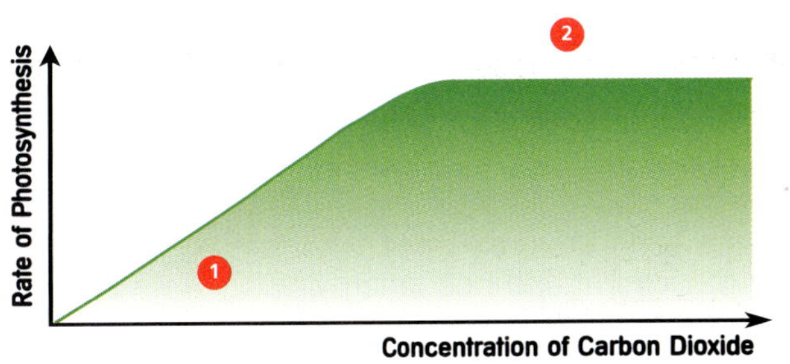

Light Intensity

1. As the light intensity increases, so does the rate of photosynthesis. Light intensity is limiting the rate of photosynthesis.
2. After reaching a certain point, an increase in light intensity has no further effect. Light intensity is no longer the limiting factor – it must be carbon dioxide or temperature.

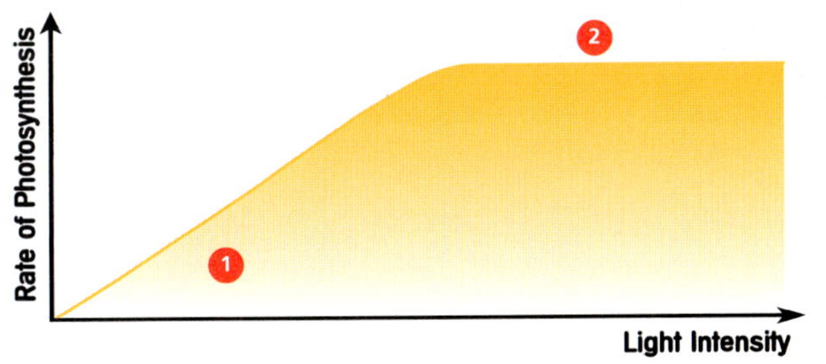

Artificial Controls

Greenhouses can be used to **control the rate** of photosynthesis. This can result in plants...

- growing more quickly
- becoming bigger and stronger.

Key Words

Chlorophyll • Mineral ions • Nitrates • Photosynthesis

Food Chains & Biomass

Food Chains

Radiation from the Sun is the source of **energy** for all **communities** of living organisms.

In green plants, photosynthesis captures a **small fraction** of the solar energy which reaches them.

This energy is stored in the substances which make up the cells of the plant. It can then be passed onto organisms which eat the plant. This transfer of energy can be represented by a **food chain**.

Pyramid of Biomass

Biomass is the mass of living materials. In a food chain, the biomass at each stage is **less** than it was at the previous stage. The biomass at each stage can be drawn to scale and shown as a **pyramid of biomass**.

Biomass and energy are **lost** at every stage of a food chain. This is due to...

- materials and energy being lost in an organism's faeces (waste)
- energy released through **respiration** being lost in movement and heat energy.

Mammals and birds, in particular, lose a lot of biomass. They must keep their body temperature constant, and higher than their surroundings.

In the biomass pyramid:

- Only a small amount of the Sun's energy is captured by the producers.
- Rabbits respire and produce waste products. They pass on $\frac{1}{10}$ of the energy they get from the grass.
- Stoats respire and produce waste products. They pass on $\frac{1}{10}$ of the energy they get from the rabbits.
- The fox gets the last bit of energy and biomass.

Since the loss of energy and biomass is due mainly to **heat loss, waste** and **movement**, the efficiency of **food production** can be improved by...

- reducing the number of stages in a food chain
- limiting an animal's movement
- controlling an animal's temperature.

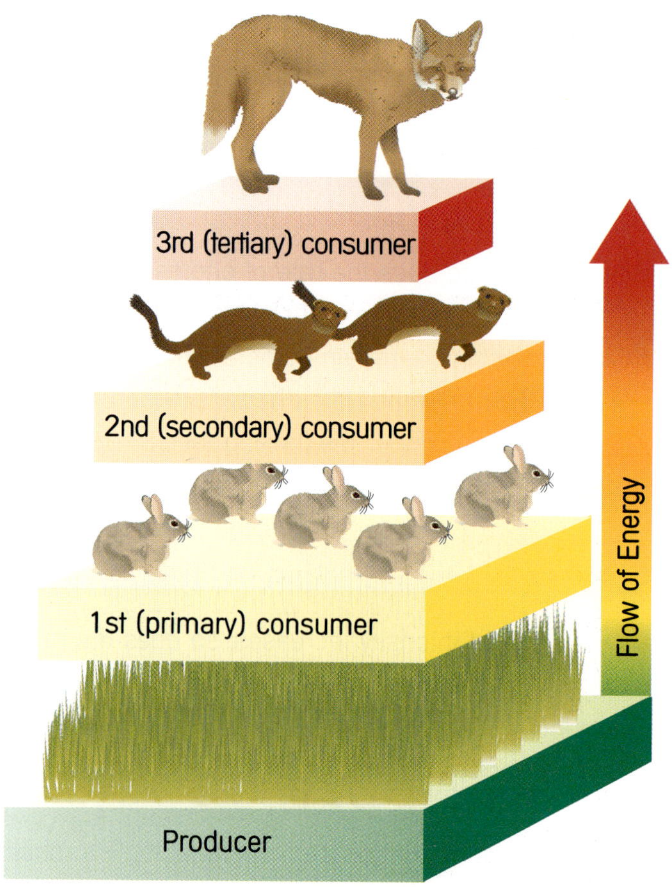

Key Words

Biomass • Carbon cycle • Community • Decay • Detritus • Environment • Food chain • Microorganisms • Photosynthesis • Radiation • Respiration

Recycling the Materials of Life

Living things (organisms) **remove materials** from the **environment** for growth and other processes.

When the organisms die or excrete waste, the materials are **returned** to the environment.

Microorganisms break down waste and dead bodies. This **decay process** releases substances needed by plants for growth.

Microorganisms digest materials faster in conditions that are **warm**, **moist** and have plenty of **oxygen**.

Microorganisms are used in...

- sewage works to break down **human waste**
- compost heaps to break down **plant material**.

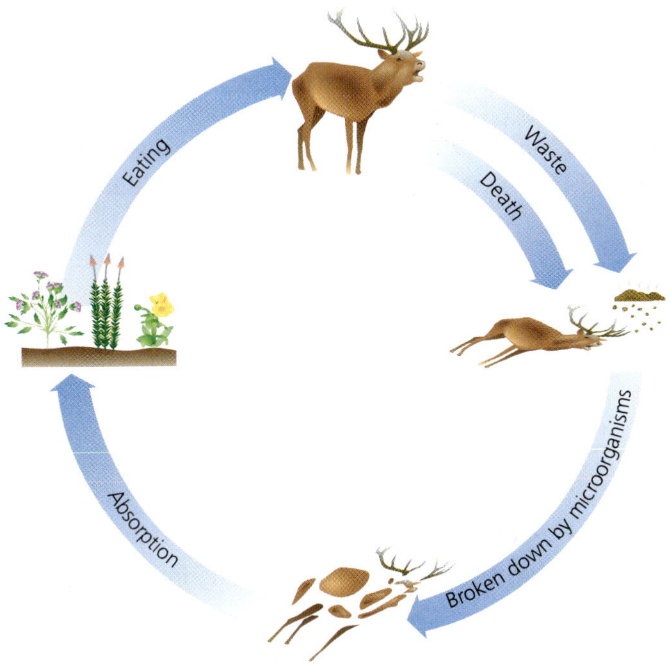

The Carbon Cycle

In a stable community, two processes are **balanced**:

- the **removal** of materials from the environment
- the **return** of materials to the environment.

This constant recycling of carbon material is called the **carbon cycle**.

1. Carbon dioxide, CO_2, is **removed** from the atmosphere by green plants for **photosynthesis**. Some CO_2 is **returned** to the atmosphere by plants during **respiration**.
2. The carbon obtained by photosynthesis is used by **plants** to make carbohydrates, fats and proteins. The plants are eaten by **animals**. Some of the carbon becomes fats and proteins in the animals.
3. Animals **respire**, releasing CO_2 into the **atmosphere**.
4. Plants and animals **die**. Other animals and microorganisms feed on their bodies, causing them to **break down**.
5. **Detritus** feeders and microorganisms respire, releasing CO_2 into the atmosphere.

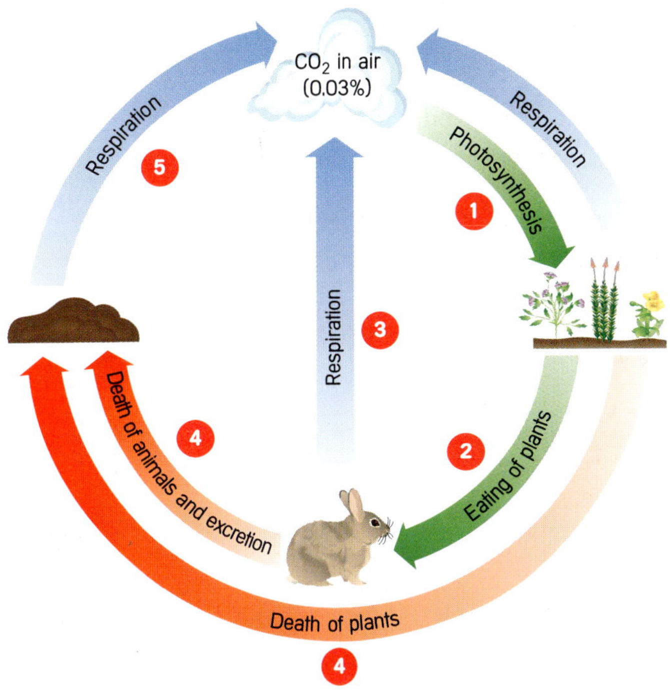

Enzymes

Enzymes

Enzymes are **biological catalysts**. They increase the rate of chemical reactions in an organism.

Enzymes are **protein** molecules, made up of long chains of **amino acids**. The chains are folded in a 3-D shape. This shape allows other molecules to fit into the enzyme.

The **shape** of the enzyme is **vital** for the enzyme's **function**. **High temperatures destroy** most enzymes' special shape. This is why it's dangerous for your body temperature to go much above 37°C.

Different enzymes work best at certain temperatures and pH levels.

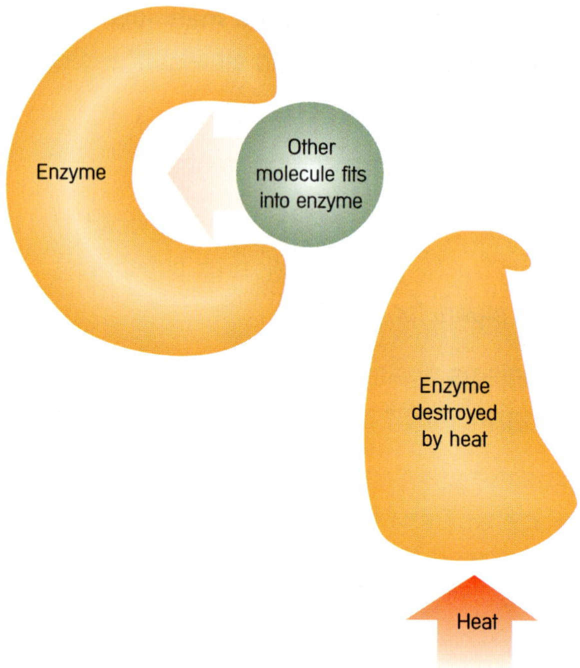

Aerobic Respiration

Aerobic respiration takes place **using oxygen**. This type of respiration…

- releases energy through the breakdown of glucose molecules
- mostly takes place inside mitochondria.

The written equation for aerobic respiration is:

Glucose + Oxygen —(catalysed by enzymes)→ **Carbon dioxide + Water (+Energy)**

Enzymes Inside Living Cells

Enzymes in living cells catalyse (speed up) processes such as…

- respiration
- protein synthesis
- photosynthesis.

The energy released during respiration is used to…

- build larger **molecules** using smaller ones
- enable **muscles** to contract (in animals)
- **maintain a constant temperature** (in mammals and birds)
- **make proteins** in plants from amino acids (from sugars and nitrates).

N.B. They all begin with M, so remember the four 'M's.

Molecules such as sugar and nitrates —(enzyme A catalyses)→ **Amino acids** —(enzyme B catalyses)→ **Protein**

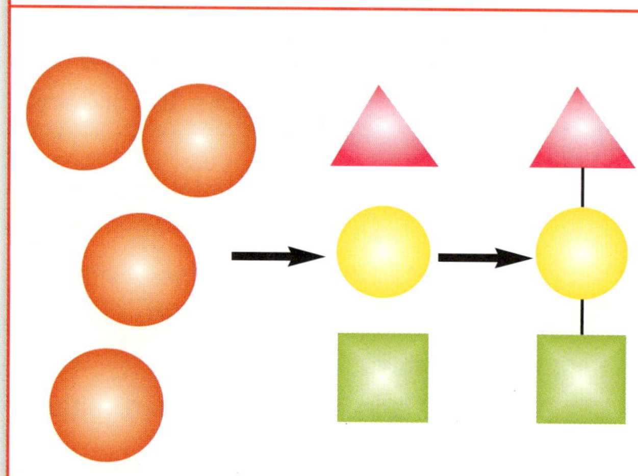

Enzymes Outside Living Cells

Some enzymes work **outside** the body cells. **Digestive enzymes** are produced by **specialised** cells in glands in the digestive system.

The enzymes...
1. Pass out of the cells into the digestive system.
2. Come into contact with food molecules.
3. Catalyse the breakdown of large food molecules into smaller molecules.

Three enzymes (**protease**, **lipase**, and **amylase**) are produced in four separate regions of the digestive system (**salivary glands**, **stomach**, **pancreas**, and **small intestine**).

The enzymes **digest** proteins, fats and carbohydrates to produce **smaller molecules** which can be **absorbed**.

Amylase...
- is produced in the salivary glands, pancreas and small intestine
- digests starch
- produces sugars.

Protease...
- is produced in the stomach, pancreas and small intestine
- digests proteins
- produces amino acids.

Lipase...
- is produced in the pancreas and small intestine
- digests lipids (fats and oils)
- produces fatty acids and glycerol.

Salivary Glands

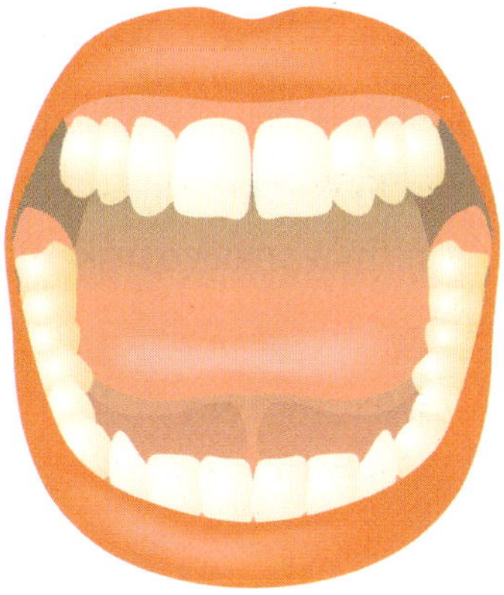

Stomach
Also produces hydrochloric acid in which these enzymes work best.

Pancreas
Produces enzymes that are released into the small intestine.

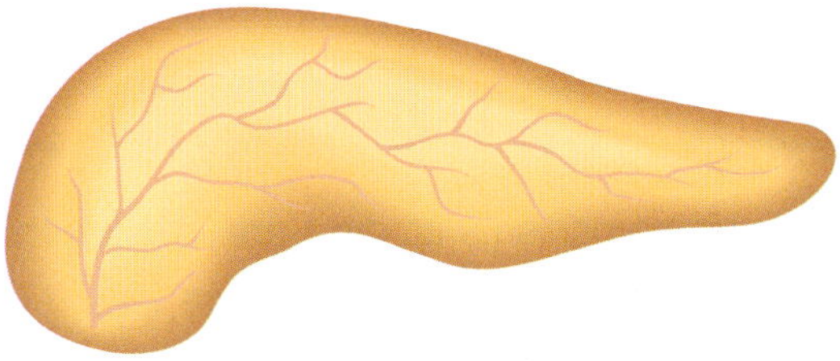

Small Intestine

Key Words

Aerobic respiration • Amylase • Catalyst • Enzyme • Lipase • Protease • Specialised

Enzymes

Bile

Bile is **produced** in your **liver**. It is **stored** in your **gall bladder** before being released into your **small intestine**.

Bile has two functions:

- **It neutralises the acid** which is added to food in your stomach. This produces alkaline conditions in which the **enzymes** of the small intestine work best.
- **It emulsifies fats** (breaks down large drops of fat into small droplets to increase their surface area). This enables the **lipase** enzymes to work much faster.

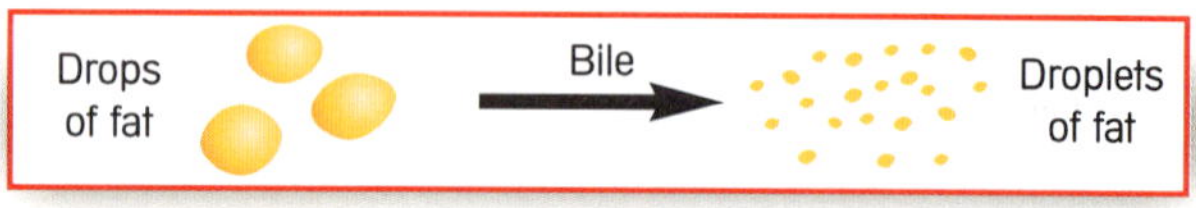

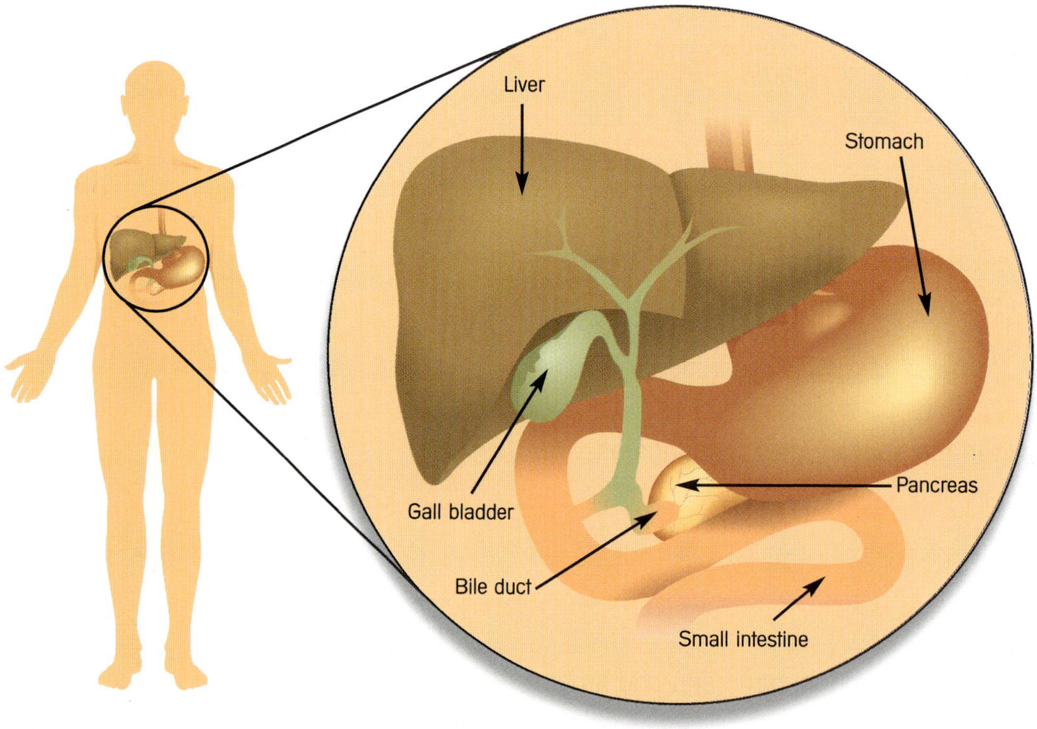

Use of Enzymes

Some microorganisms produce enzymes which can be used to our benefit both **in the home** and **in industry**.

In the home, biological detergents may contain...

- **protein-digesting** (protease) enzymes, to break down blood and food stains
- **fat-digesting** (lipase) enzymes, to break down oil and grease stains.

In industry, various enzymes are used, such as...

- **proteases**, to pre-digest protein in baby foods
- **carbohydrases**, to convert starch into sugar syrup
- **isomerase**, to convert glucose syrup into fructose syrup.

Controlling Body Conditions

Controlling Body Conditions

In order to function properly, your body has to control levels of...

- blood sugar
- water content
- **ion** content
- temperature.

Blood Glucose Concentration

Blood glucose concentration is monitored and controlled by the **pancreas** which secretes the hormone **insulin**.

The level of insulin in the pancreas affects what happens in the **liver**. The pancreas...

- continually monitors the body's blood sugar levels
- adjusts the amount of insulin released in order to keep the body's blood sugar levels as close to normal as possible.

If the pancreas doesn't produce enough insulin, a person's blood glucose concentration may rise to a fatally high level.

This is a condition called **diabetes**, which can be controlled by...

- careful attention to diet
- injecting insulin into the blood.

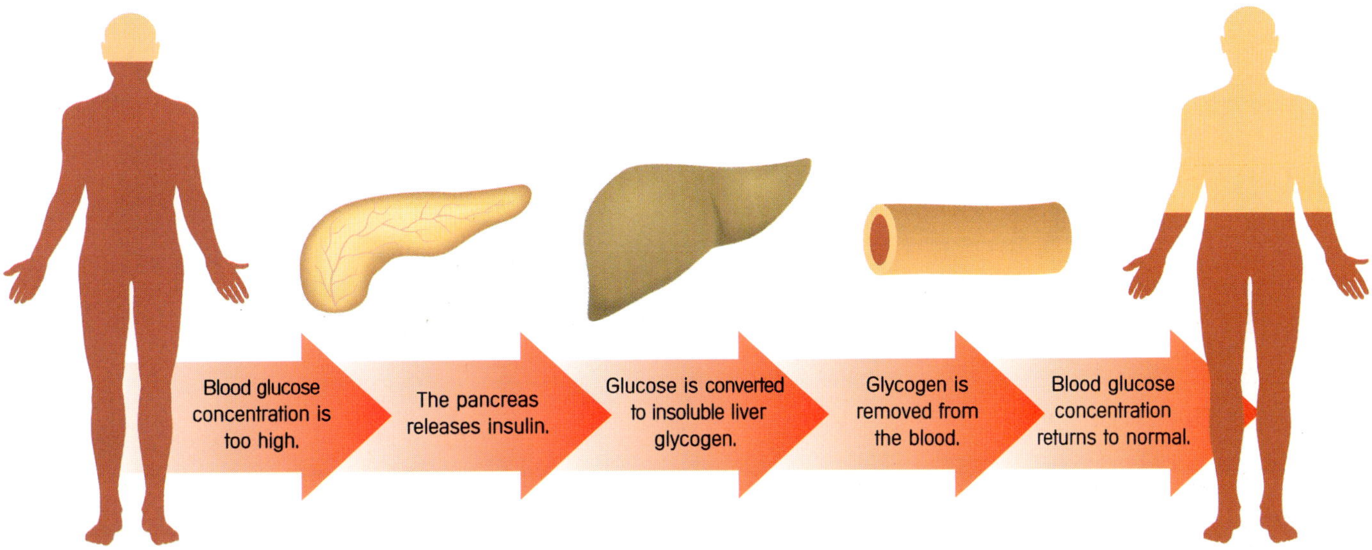

Water and Ion Content

If the **water** or **ion content** of the body is wrong, too much water may move into or out of the cells by **osmosis**. This can cause damage to the cells.

Your body gains water and ions through food and drink.

Key Words

Bile • Diabetes • Enzyme • Insulin • Ion • Osmosis

Body Temperature

Body Temperature

Your body temperature is **monitored** and **controlled** by the **thermoregulatory centre** in the brain. This centre has receptors that are sensitive to the temperature of blood flowing through them.

Temperature receptors in the skin also provide information about skin temperature. Sweat helps to cool your body when it is **hot**. More water is **lost** from the body, so more water has to be **taken** in as food or drink to balance this.

Your body temperature should be kept at around 37°C.

HT Hot Conditions:

If your core body temperature becomes too **high**…

- blood vessels in skin **dilate** (become wide), increasing heat loss
- sweat glands release **sweat** which evaporates, causing cooling.

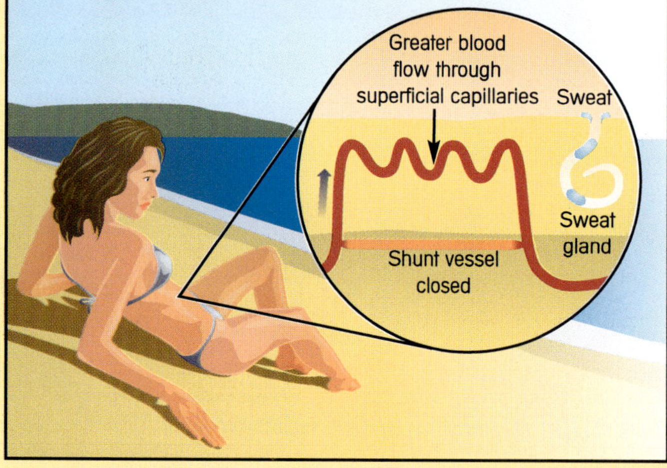

Cold Conditions:

If your core body temperature becomes too **low**…

- blood vessels in skin **constrict** (become narrower), reducing heat loss
- muscles start to **'shiver'** causing heat energy to be released by respiration in cells.

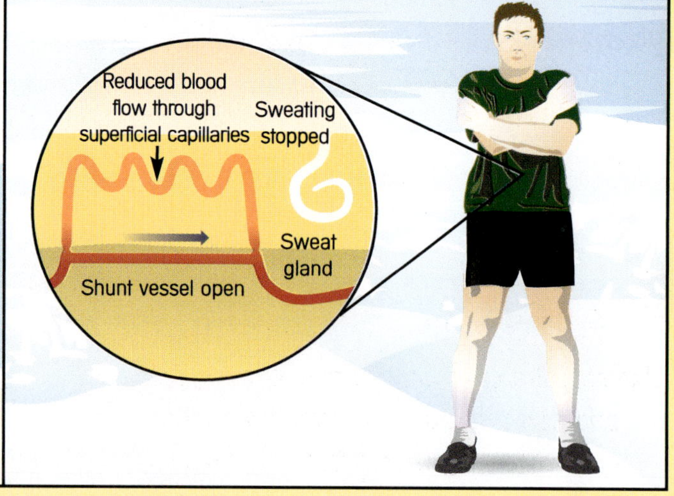

Removing Waste Products

You need to **remove waste products** from your body to keep your internal environment relatively **constant**.

Two of these waste products are…

- **carbon dioxide** – produced by **respiration** and removed through the lungs during exhalation
- **urea** – produced by the liver when it breaks down amino acids, removed by the kidneys, and temporarily stored in the bladder.

Chromosomes & Gametes

Human Body Cells

Body cells contain **46 chromosomes** arranged as **23 pairs**.

Gametes are sex cells, i.e. female eggs and male sperm. Gametes have **23 chromosomes** (one from each pair).

The fusion of two gamete cells produces a **zygote**. A zygote has 46 chromosomes in total (23 pairs).

Pairs of Chromosomes in a Male

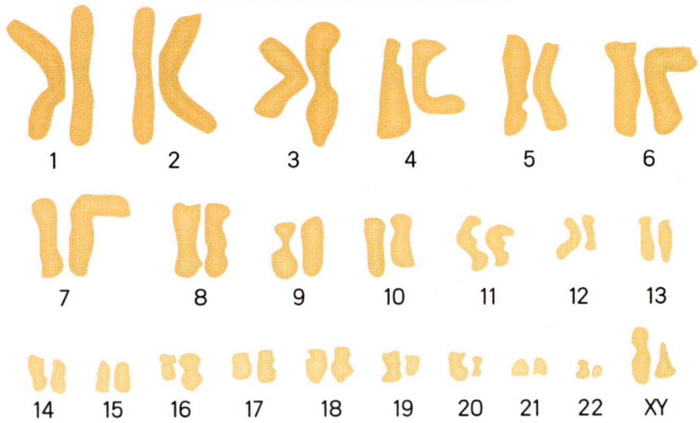

Inheritance of the Sex Chromosome

Of the 23 pairs of chromosomes in the human body, 1 pair contains the **sex chromosomes**.

- **In females**, these chromosomes are identical and are called the X chromosomes.
- **In males**, one chromosome (Y) is much shorter than the other (X).

Female Sex Chromosomes	Male Sex Chromosomes
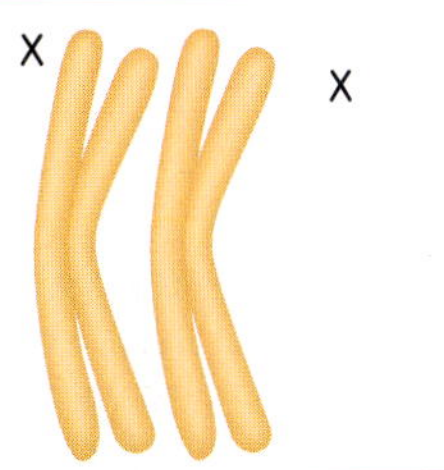	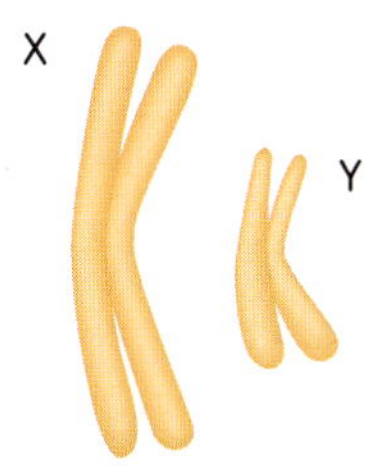

Like all pairs of chromosomes, offspring inherit...

- one sex chromosome from the mother
- one sex chromosome from the father.

So, the sex of an individual is ultimately decided by whether the ovum is fertilised by an **X-carrying sperm** or a **Y-carrying sperm**.

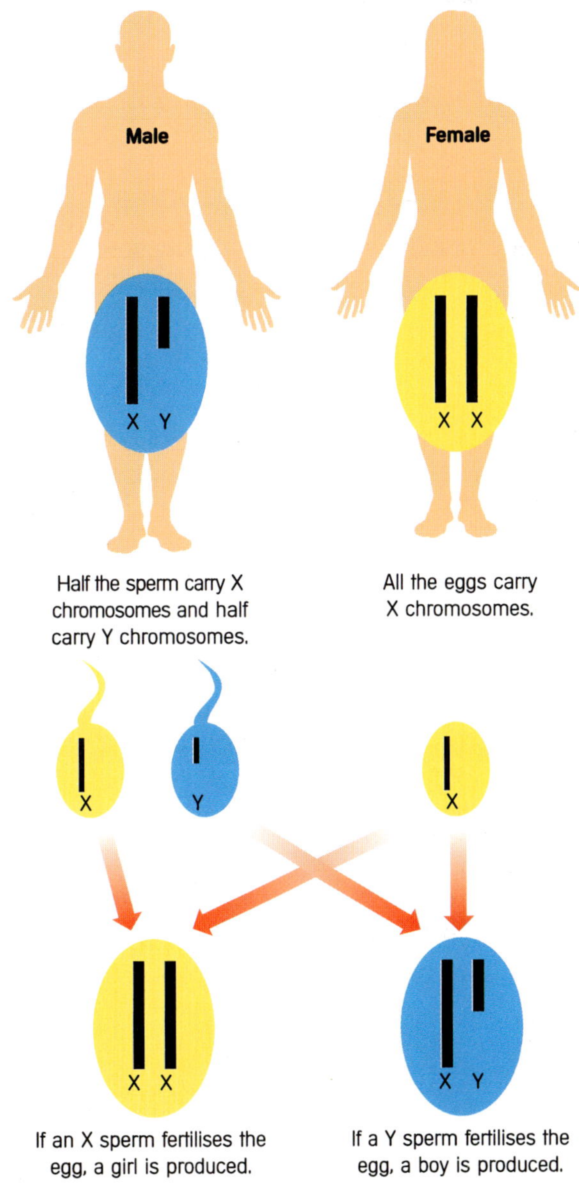

Key Words

Chromosome • Gamete • Respiration • Thermoregulation • Urea • Zygote

Cell Division

Mitosis

Mitosis is the **division** of body cells to produce new cells. Mitosis occurs...

- for growth
- for repair
- in asexual reproduction.

Before the cell divides, a copy of each chromosome is made. The **new cell** contains exactly the **same genetic information** as the **parent** cell, i.e. the same number of chromosomes and the same genes.

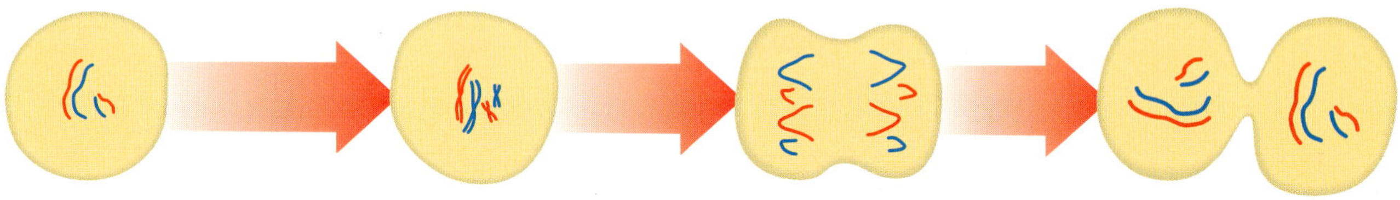

Parent cell with two pairs of chromosomes. | Each chromosome replicates itself. | The copies are pulled apart. Cell now divides for the only time. | Two 'daughter' cells are formed.

HT Meiosis

Meiosis occurs in the **testes** and **ovaries**. The cells in these organs divide to produce the gametes (eggs and sperm) for sexual reproduction.

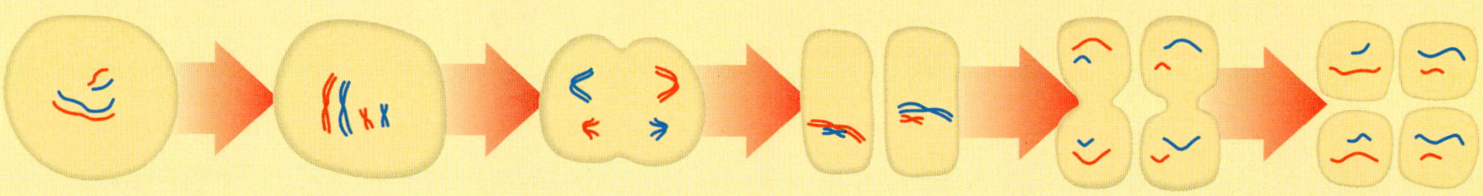

Cell with two pairs of chromosomes. | Each chromosome replicates itself. | Chromosomes part company and move to opposite sides with their 'copies'. | Cell divides for the first time. | Copies now separate and the second cell division takes place. | Four gametes, each with half the number of chromosomes of the parent cell.

Fertilisation

During **fertilisation**, the female and male gametes join. One chromosome comes from each parent. A **single body cell** with **new pairs** of chromosomes is formed. The cell then divides repeatedly by **mitosis** to form a new individual, giving rise to **variation**.

Egg | Sperm | Fertilisation | First cell of new individual | Development of new individual

Alleles

Some **genes** have different forms or variations, called **alleles**. For example...

- the gene that controls tongue-rolling ability has two alleles – you either can or you can't
- the gene that controls eye colour has two alleles – blue or brown.

In a pair of chromosomes, the alleles for a gene can be the **same** or **different**. If they are different, then one allele will be **dominant** and one allele will be **recessive**.

A dominant allele **will control** the characteristics of the gene. Dominant alleles express themselves even if present on only one chromosome. So, in the example of brown eyes, an individual can be...

- **homozygous dominant** (BB)
- **heterozygous** (Bb).

A recessive allele will **only** control the characteristics of the gene if it is present on **both chromosomes in a pair** (i.e. no dominant allele is present). So, in the example of blue eyes, an individual can only be **homozygous recessive** (bb).

Example: Dominant and Recessive Alleles
The diagram shows three pairs of genes from the middle of a pair of chromosomes. The genes code for...

- tongue-rolling ability
- eye colour
- type of earlobe (i.e. attached or unattached).

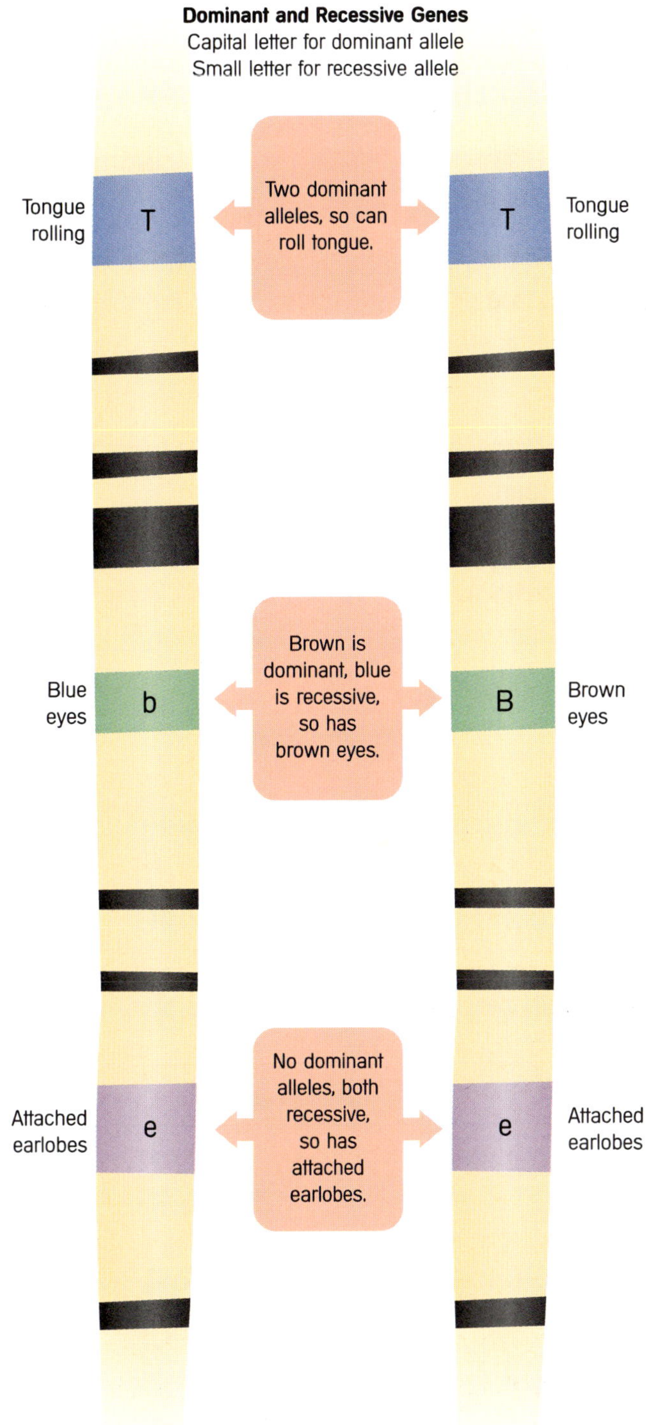

Key Words

Allele • Fertilisation • Gene • Meiosis • Mitosis

	Homozygous Dominant	Heterozygous	Homozygous Recessive
Tongue rolling	TT (can roll)	Tt (can roll)	tt (can't roll)
Eye colour	BB (brown)	Bb (brown)	bb (blue)
Earlobes	EE (free earlobes)	Ee (free earlobes)	ee (attached earlobes)

Genetic Diagrams

Monohybrid Inheritance

When a characteristic is determined by **just one pair of alleles** then a simple **genetic cross diagram** can be drawn to show inheritance of genes.

This type of inheritance is referred to as **monohybrid inheritance**.

Inheritance of Eye Colour

In genetic diagrams you should use **capital letters for dominant alleles** and **lower case letters for recessive alleles**. So, for eye colour, 'B' is used for brown eye alleles and 'b' is used for blue eye alleles.

From the crosses on the diagrams, the following can be seen:

1. If one parent has two dominant genes then **all the offspring** will inherit that characteristic.

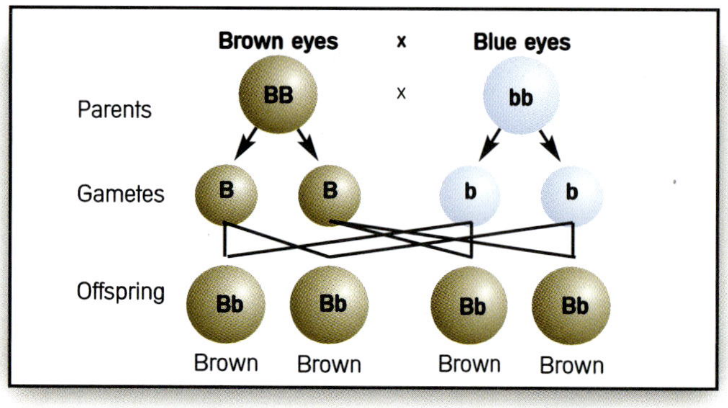

2. If both parents have one recessive gene then this characteristic **may** appear in the offspring (25% chance).

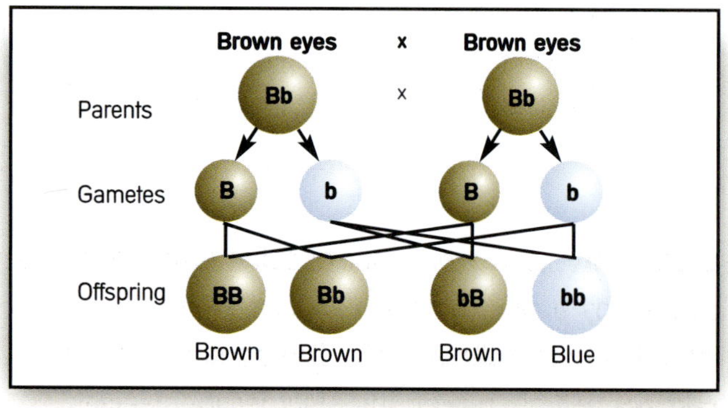

3. If one parent has one recessive gene and the other has two recessive genes, then there is a 50% chance of that characteristic appearing in the offspring.

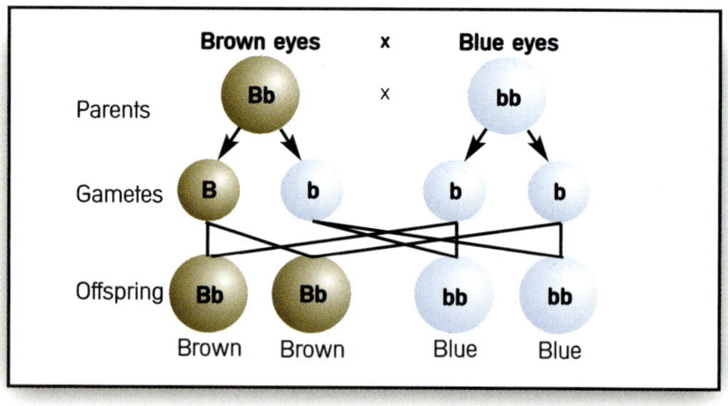

But remember, these are **only probabilities**. In practice, all that matters is which egg is fertilised by which sperm. This process is completely **random**.

HT When you construct genetic diagrams remember to...

- clearly **identify** the alleles of the parents
- place each of these alleles in a **separate gamete**
- **join** each gamete with the two gametes from the other parent.

Differentiation of Cells

Differentiation is when cells develop a **specialised** structure to carry out a specific function.

- Most plant cells can differentiate throughout life.
- Animal cells **can only** differentiate at an early stage.
- Mature animal cells divide for repair / replacement.

Chromosomes, DNA & Genes

Stem Cells

Stem cells are cells in human **embryos** and adult **bone marrow** which have **not yet differentiated**.

They can differentiate into **many different types** of cells, e.g. nerve cells. Treatment using these cells may help treat people with conditions like **paralysis**.

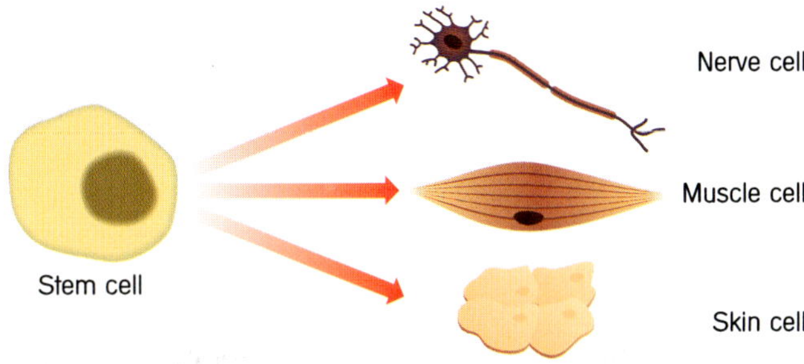

Chromosomes, DNA and Genes

Chromosomes are made up of long, coiled molecules of **DNA** (**deoxyribonucleic acid**).

A DNA molecule consists of **two strands** which are coiled to form a **double helix**.

Each person has **unique** DNA (apart from identical twins). So, DNA can be used for **identification** (DNA fingerprinting).

A **gene** is a small section of DNA. Genes code for a particular inherited characteristic, e.g. blue eyes.

HT Genes code for a particular characteristic by providing a code for a combination of amino acids which make up a protein.

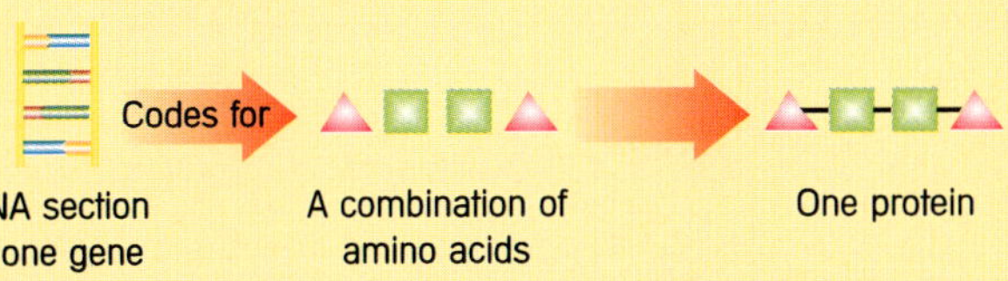

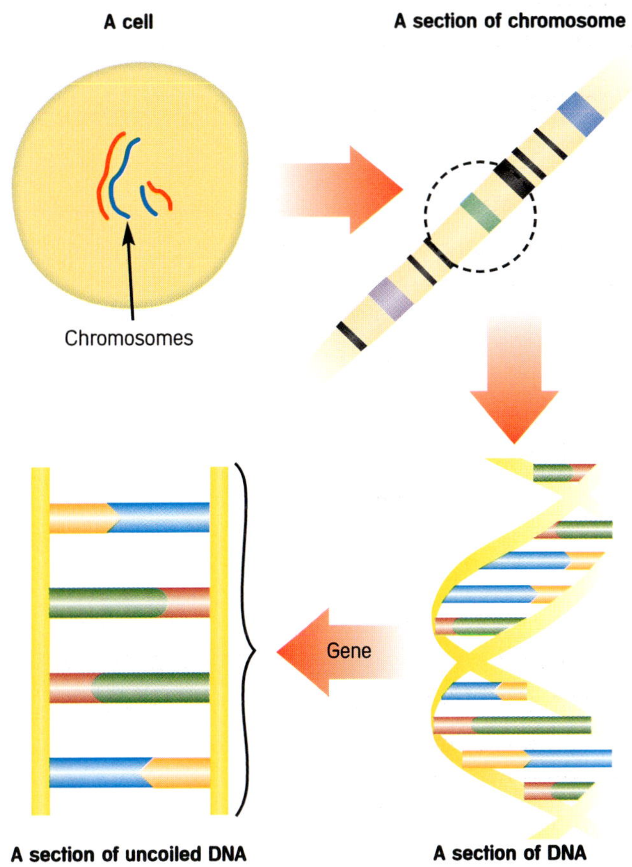

Genetic Disorders

Embryos can be screened for the genes that cause genetic disorders, such as...

- Huntington's disease
- Cystic fibrosis.

Huntington's disease is a disorder of the nervous system caused by a **dominant allele**. It can be passed on even if only **one parent** has the disorder.

Cystic fibrosis is a disorder of cell membranes. It is caused by a **recessive allele**. So, it must be inherited from **both parents**. The parents can be **carriers** without having the disorder themselves.

Key Words

Allele • Differentiation • DNA • Gene • Specialised • Stem cell

Biology Unit 2 Summary

Cells

The structure of cells is related to their **function**. Cells may be **specialised** to carry out a particular job.

Animal and plants cells have a nucleus, cytoplasm, cell membrane, mitochondria and ribosomes.

Plant cells also have a cell wall, chloroplasts and a permanent vacuole.

Diffusion = movement of **particles** from high to low concentration.

Osmosis = movement of **water** from high to low concentration.

Plant Growth

Green plants **make** their own **food** using **sunlight**. This process is called **photosynthesis**.

$$\textbf{Carbon dioxide} + \textbf{Water} \xrightarrow[\text{chlorophyll}]{\text{light}} \textbf{Glucose} + \textbf{Oxygen}$$

Rate of photosynthesis is limited by **temperature, carbon dioxide concentration** and **light intensity**.

Plants need to **absorb mineral ions** (nitrates and magnesium) for healthy growth.

Food Chains and Biomass

A **food chain** represents the **transfer of energy** from organism to organism.

Pyramids of biomass show the mass of **living materials** at each stage of the food chain. Biomass is **lost** at each stage.

Recycling Materials

Living things **remove materials** from the environment. These materials are **returned** to the environment when the organisms die or excrete waste.

The **carbon cycle** is the constant **recycling** of carbon material.

Aerobic Respiration

Aerobic respiration takes place **using oxygen**.

$$\textbf{Glucose} + \textbf{Oxygen} \xrightarrow[\text{by enzymes}]{\text{catalysed}} \textbf{Carbon dioxide} + \textbf{Water} \quad \textbf{(+ Energy)}$$

Biology Unit 2 Summary

Enzymes

Enzymes are **biological catalysts**. **Inside** body cells, enzymes **speed up** reactions such as respiration, protein synthesis and photosynthesis.

Outside body cells, digestive enzymes are produced in the digestive system.

Bile, produced in the liver, neutralises acid and emulsifies fats.

Enzyme	Where Produced
Amylase	• Salivary glands • Pancreas • Small intestine
Protease	• Stomach • Small intestine
Lipase	• Pancreas • Small intestine

Controlling Body Conditions

The human body has to control the levels of blood sugar, water, ion content and temperature.

Diabetes = a condition in which the pancreas isn't able to control the levels of insulin in the body.

Body temperature is monitored and controlled by the **thermoregulatory** centre in the brain.

HT

Body temperature	Body Reaction
Too high	• Blood vessels dilate • Sweat glands release sweat
Too low	• Blood vessels constrict • Muscles start to shiver causing heat energy to be released.

Human Body Cells

Human body cells → **46 chromosomes** → 23 pairs

Gametes → sex cells → 23 chromosomes

Two gametes join to produce a **zygote** with 46 chromosomes.

DNA → Gene → Chromosome

Alleles = variations of genes.

Dominant alleles – control gene characteristics if present **once**. **Recessive** alleles – only control gene characteristics if present **twice**.

Differentiation – cells carry out a specific function. Stem cells have not yet differentiated.

Mitosis

Mitosis = **division** of body cells to produce new cells. The new cells contain **identical genetic** information to that of the parent cell.

After **fertilisation**, a zygote divides repeatedly by mitosis to form a new individual.

HT **Meiosis** = division of cells in the testes and ovaries to produce gametes. The gametes will have half the number of chromosomes as the parent cell.

Biology Practice Questions

1. The diagram shows a human cheek cell.

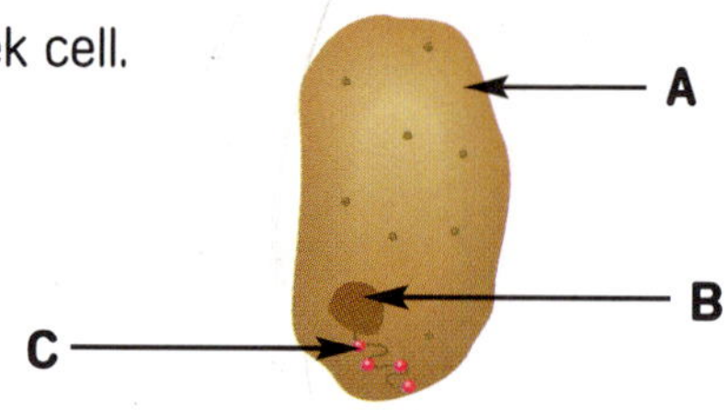

a) Give the names of the parts labelled A to C.

A .... **B** .... **C** ....

b) Explain what happens in mitochondria.

....

c) Which structure controls the passage of substances in and out of the cell? ....

2. **a)** Name four things that a plant needs for the process of photosynthesis.

i) .... **ii)** ....

iii) .... **iv)** ....

b) Name the two products of photosynthesis.

i) .... **ii)** ....

c) Name the process in which...

i) gases pass in and out of plant cells ....

ii) water passes from the soil to the roots. ....

d) What physical change would you expect to see in a plant that is deficient in magnesium ions?

....

3. Clare noticed a blackbird, sitting in an oak tree, eating ladybirds. When she looked closer she saw that there were greenfly on the leaves of the tree, and the greenfly were being eaten by the ladybirds.

The diagram below represents the pyramid of biomass relating to the food chain above. Write the name of each organism in the correct place at the side of each stage.

A ....

B ....

C ....

D ....

4 This question has two parts. For each part, tick the correct answer.

a) Which organ in the human body monitors blood sugar concentration?

i) The liver ☐ **ii)** The pancreas ☐

iii) The kidneys ☐ **iv)** The gall bladder ☐

b) If the body is unable to produce enough insulin naturally, what could happen to blood glucose concentration?

i) It could rise a little ☐ **ii)** It could drop ☐

iii) It could rise to a fatally high level ☐ **iv)** It could stay the same ☐

5 Biological catalysts are enzymes which speed up chemical reactions in an organism.

a) Give two processes inside living cells that enzymes could speed up.

i) .... **ii)** ....

b) Name two factors that can change the effectiveness of enzymes.

i) .... **ii)** ....

c) Describe the functions of bile.

....

6 There are several parts to this question. For each part, tick the correct answer.

a) Name the large molecule which forms the basis of chromosomes.

i) Gene ☐ **ii)** Alleles ☐

iii) DNA ☐ **iv)** Gametes ☐

b) How many chromosomes are there in a normal human sperm?

i) 22 ☐ **ii)** 23 ☐

iii) 46 ☐ **iv)** 50 ☐

HT **c)** Nick is homozygous dominant for brown eyes and Claire is homozygous recessive for blue eyes. Nick and Claire have a child. What is the percentage chance of their child having brown eyes?

i) 25% ☐ **ii)** 50% ☐

iii) 75% ☐ **iv)** 100% ☐

Atoms

Atoms

Atoms have a small central nucleus which is made up of **protons** and **neutrons**. The **nucleus** is surrounded by **electrons**.

Protons, neutrons and electrons have relative **electrical charges**.

Atomic Particle	Relative Charge
Proton	+1
Neutron	0
Electron	-1

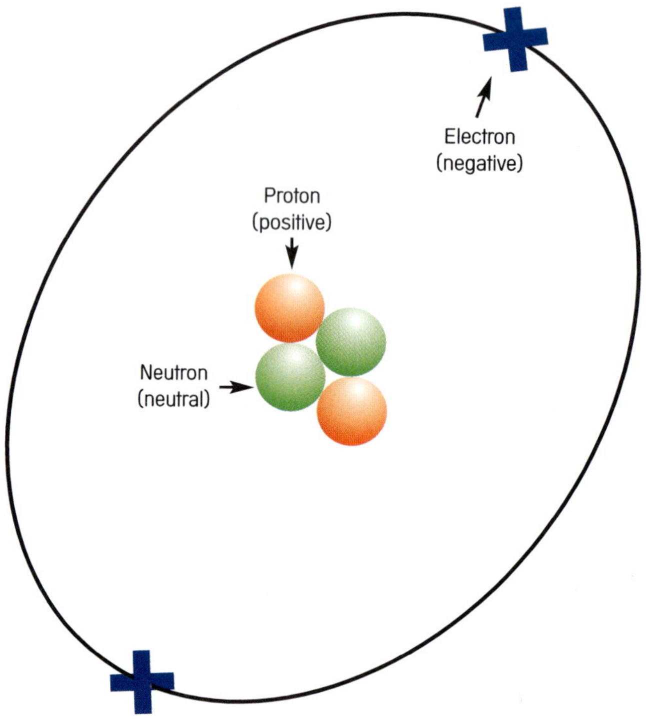

Atoms as a whole have **no overall charge** as they contain an **equal number** of **protons** and **electrons**.

All atoms of a particular element have the **same number of protons**. Atoms of different elements have **different numbers of protons**. The number of protons in an atom is called its **atomic number**.

Elements are arranged in the modern periodic table in order of **atomic number**.

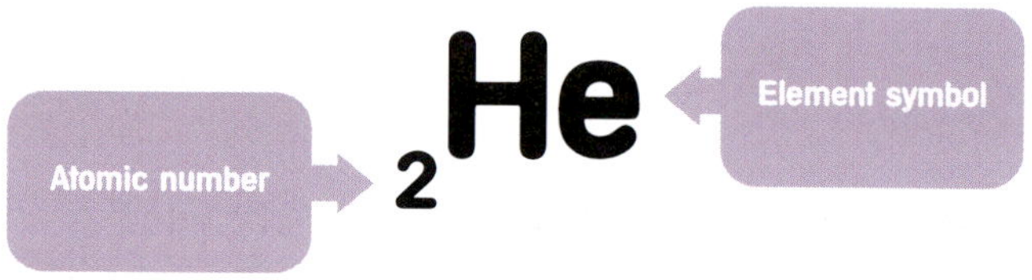

Electron Configuration and Structure

Electrons in an atom occupy the lowest available **energy level** (i.e. the innermost available shell).

- The **first** level can only contain a **maximum** of **2 electrons**.
- The energy levels after this can each hold a **maximum** of **8 electrons**.

The **electron configuration** tells us how the electrons are arranged around the nucleus in **energy levels** or **shells**. It is written as a series of numbers, for example...

- oxygen is 2,6
- aluminium is 2,8,3

The **periodic table** groups together the elements in terms of **electronic structure**.

Elements in the **same group** have the same number of **electrons** in their **highest energy level** (**outer shell**). They also have **similar properties**.

A particular energy level is gradually filled with electrons from **left to right**, across each **period**.

Key Words

Atomic number • Compound • Covalent bond • Electron • Ionic bond • Neutron • Nucleus • Proton

Alkali Metals & Halogens

The Alkali Metals (Group 1)

The alkali metals...

- have 1 electron in their outermost shell
- react with **non-metal elements** to form **ionic compounds** where the metal ion has a single **positive** charge.

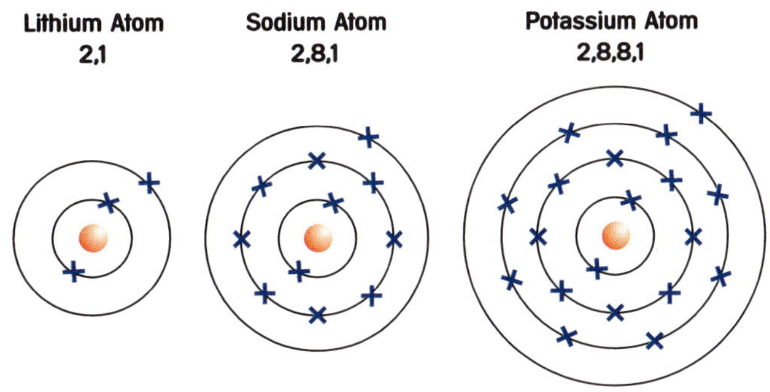

The Halogens (Group 7)

The halogens...

- have 7 electrons in their outermost shell
- react with **alkali metals** to form **ionic compounds** where the halide ions have a single **negative** charge.

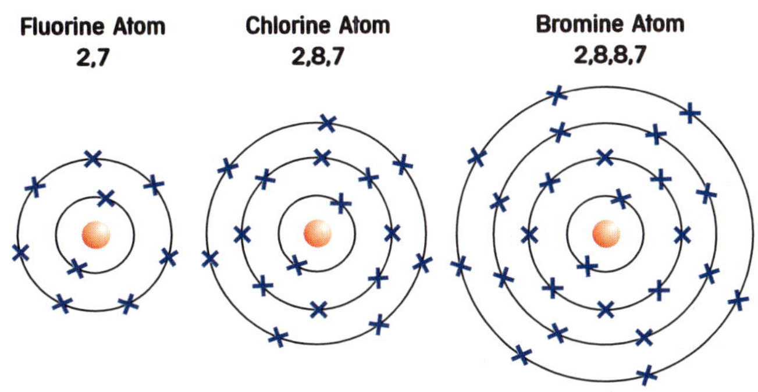

Mixtures and Compounds

A **mixture** consists of two or more elements or **compounds** that are **not chemically combined**. The properties of the substances remain unchanged and specific to that substance.

Compounds are substances in which the atoms of two or more elements **are chemically combined** (not just mixed together).

Atoms can form chemical bonds by...

- **sharing electrons** (**covalent bonds**)
- **gaining** or **losing electrons** (**ionic bonds**).

When atoms form **chemical bonds**, the arrangement of the **outer shell** of electrons **changes**. This results in each atom getting a **complete outer shell** of electrons. For most atoms this is eight electrons, but for helium it is only two.

HT Simple Molecular Compounds

Substances that consist of **simple molecules** are gases, liquids and solids that have relatively **low melting** and **boiling points**. This is because they only have weak intermolecular forces (forces between their molecules). The molecules have no overall electrical charge, so they can't conduct electricity.

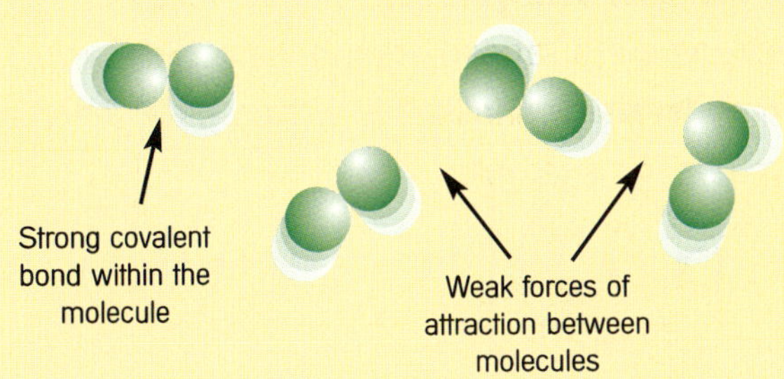

Ionic Bonding

Ionic Compounds

Ionic compounds are giant structures of **ions**. They are held together by **strong forces** of attraction (electrostatic forces) between **oppositely charged ions**, that act in **all directions**. This type of bonding is called **ionic bonding**.

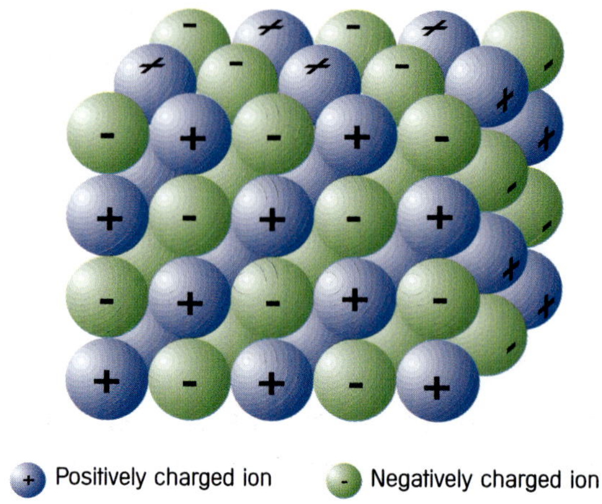

Ionic compounds...

- have **high melting** and **boiling points**
- **conduct electricity** when molten or in solution because the charged ions are free to move about and carry the current.

The Ionic Bond

An **ionic bond** occurs between a **metal** and a **non-metal** atom. It involves a **transfer** of **electrons** from one atom to the other.

This forms electrically charged **ions**, each of which has a complete outer energy level.

They have the electronic structure of a noble gas.

- Atoms which **lose electrons** become **positively** charged ions.
- Atoms which **gain electrons** become **negatively** charged ions.

Example 1

Sodium (Na) and chlorine (Cl) bond ionically to form sodium chloride, NaCl.

1. The sodium atom has 1 electron in its outer shell.
2. The electron is transferred to the chlorine atom.
3. Both atoms now have 8 electrons in their outer shell.
4. The atoms become ions, Na^+ and Cl^-.
5. The compound formed is sodium chloride, NaCl.

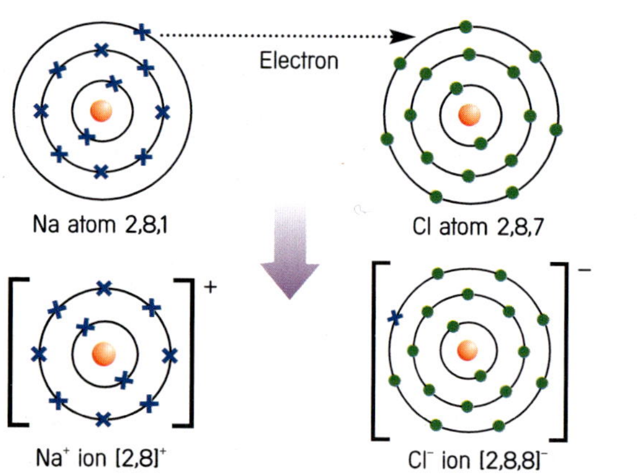

Example 2

Magnesium (Mg) and oxygen (O) bond ionically to form magnesium oxide, MgO.

1. The magnesium atom has 2 electrons in its outer shell.
2. These 2 electrons are transferred to the oxygen atom.
3. Both atoms now have 8 electrons in their outer shell.
4. The atoms become ions, Mg^{2+} and O^{2-}.
5. The compound formed is magnesium oxide, MgO.

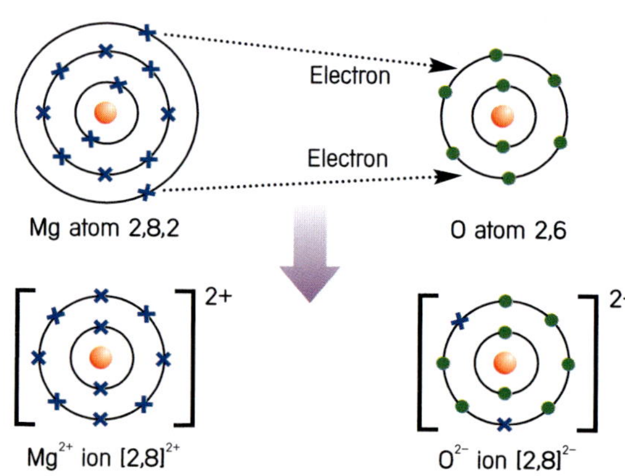

The Covalent Bond

A **covalent bond** occurs between **non-metal atoms**. It is a strong bond which is formed when **pairs of electrons are shared**.

Some covalently bonded substances have **simple bonds**, e.g. H_2, Cl_2, O_2, HCl, H_2O and CH_4.

Others have **giant covalent structures**, called **macromolecules**, e.g. diamond and silicon dioxide.

Atoms which share electrons usually have **low melting** and **boiling points**. This is because they often form molecules in which there are...

- **strong covalent bonds** between the **atoms**
- **weak forces of attraction** between the **molecules**.

Key Words

Covalent bond • Electron • Ion • Ionic bond

Example

1. A chlorine atom has 7 electrons in its outer shell.
2. In order to bond with another chlorine atom, an electron from each atom is shared.
3. This gives each chlorine atom 8 electrons in the outer shell.
4. Each atom now has a complete outer shell.

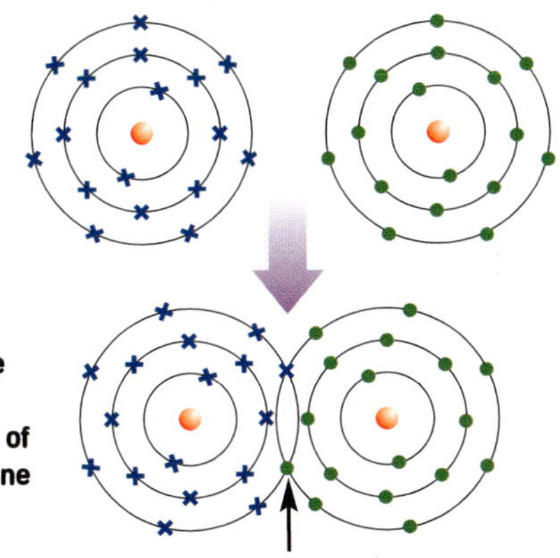

Covalent Bonding

There are three different methods for representing the covalent bonds in each molecule. You need to be familiar with the following examples, and know how to use the different methods.

The two most common forms are shown in this table:

The third form is shown here for an ammonia molecule. But, unless specifically asked for, you should use the other two methods.

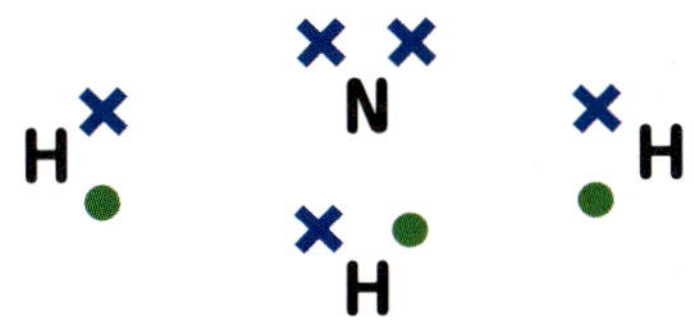

Molecule	Water H_2O	Chlorine Cl_2	Hydrogen H_2	Hydrogen chloride, HCl	Methane CH_4	Oxygen O_2
Method 1	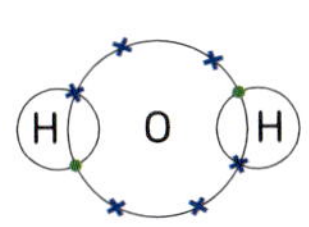	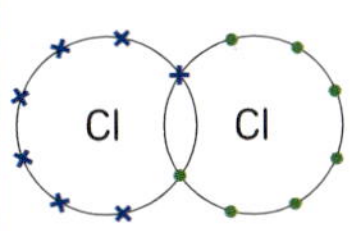	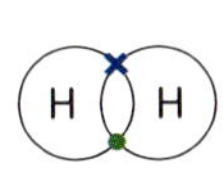	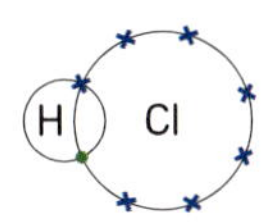	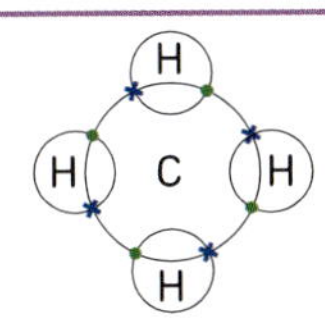	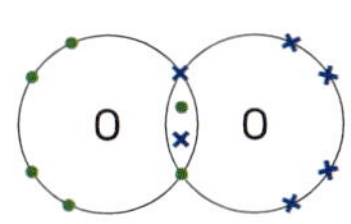
Method 2	H–O–H	Cl – Cl	H – H	H – Cl	H–C–H with H above and H below C	O = O (a double bond)

Covalent Structures

Giant Covalent Structures

All the atoms in giant covalent structures are linked by **strong covalent bonds**. This means they have very **high melting points**.

Diamond is a form of carbon that has a **giant, rigid covalent structure** (lattice). Each carbon atom forms **four covalent bonds** with other carbon atoms.

Diamond has a **large number of covalent bonds** so it is a very **hard substance**.

Graphite is a form of carbon that also has a giant covalent structure. However, in graphite, each carbon atom forms **three covalent bonds** with other carbon atoms in a layered structure.

Graphite has layers that can slide past each other, making it soft and slippery.

HT In graphite, one electron from each carbon atom is delocalised. These delocalised electrons allow graphite to **conduct heat and electricity**.

Silicon dioxide (or silica, SiO_2) has a lattice structure similar to diamond. Each **oxygen** atom is joined to **two silicon atoms**, and each **silicon** atom is joined to **four oxygen atoms**.

Diamond

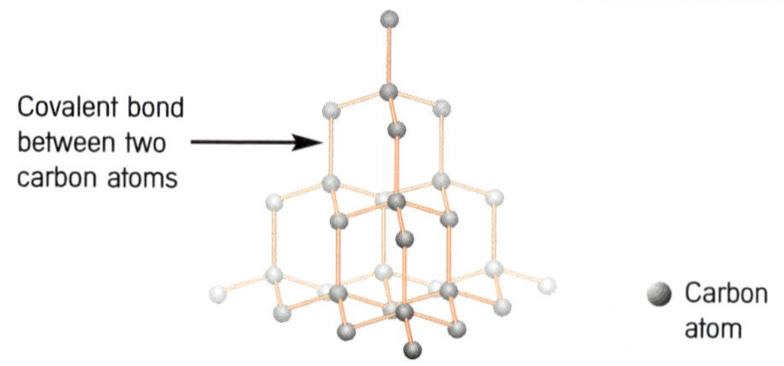

Graphite

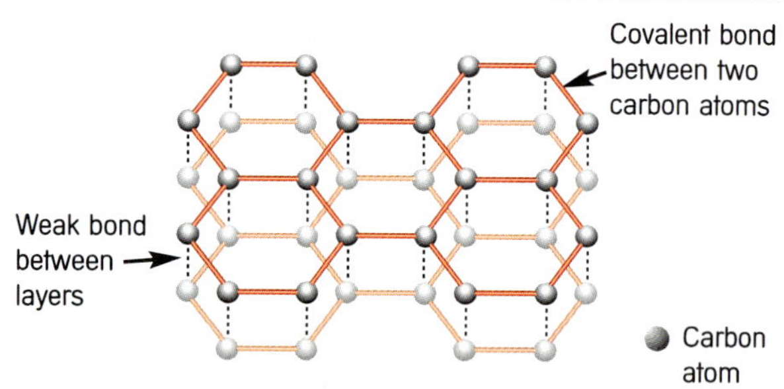

Silicon Dioxide

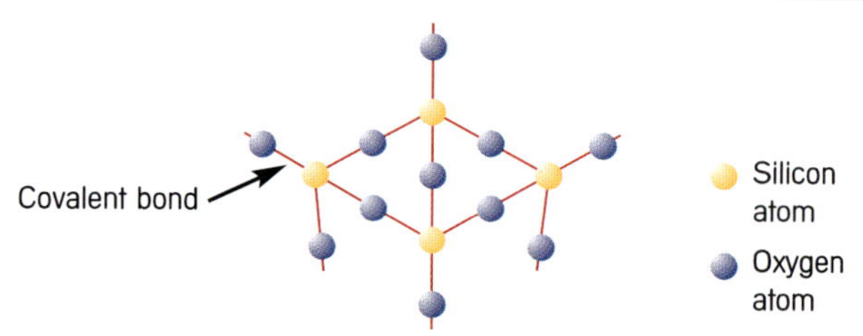

Metals

The layers of atoms in metals are able to slide over each other. This means that metals can be **bent and shaped**.

HT Metals have a giant structure in which electrons in the highest energy level can be **delocalised**.

This produces a regular arrangement (lattice) of **positive ions** that are held together by electrons using electrostatic attraction.

These delocalised electrons can move around freely. This allows metal to **conduct heat and electricity**.

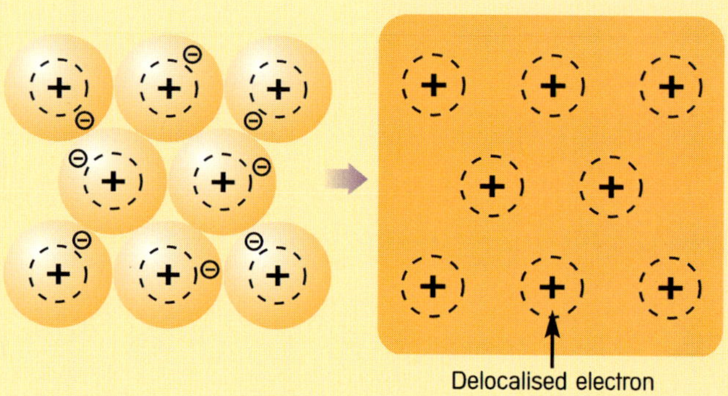

Nanoparticles and Nanostructures

Nanoscience is the study of very small structures. The structures are 1–100 nanometres in size, roughly in the order of a few hundred atoms.

One **nanometre** is 0.000 000 001 m (one billionth of a metre) and is written as 1 nm or $1\,m \times 10^{-9}$.

Nanoparticles are tiny, tiny particles that can combine to form structures called **nanostructures**.

Nanostructures can be manipulated so materials can be developed that have new and specific properties.

The **properties** of **nanoparticles** are different to the properties of the **same materials in bulk**.

For example...

- electrons can move through an insulating layer of atoms
- nanoparticles are more sensitive to light, heat and magnetism
- nanoparticles have a high surface area in relation to their volume.

Human Hair	Virus/Small Bacteria	Atoms and Small Molecules
0.000 01 metre $= 1 \times 10^{-5}$ m	0.000 000 1 metre $= 1 \times 10^{-7}$ m	0.000 000 001 metre $= 1 \times 10^{-9}$ m
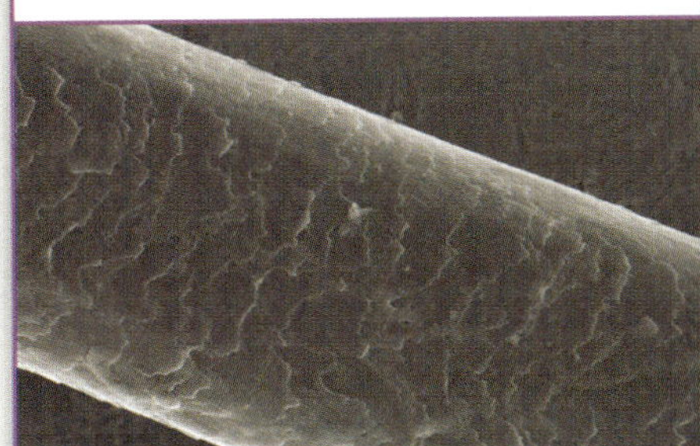		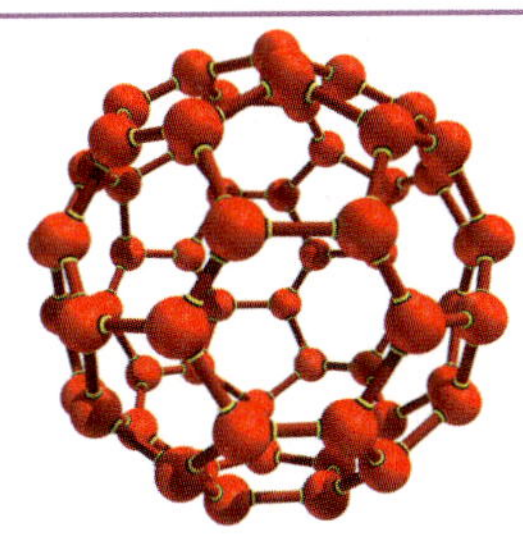
Can be seen using a microscope	Can be seen using an electron microscope	Nanoparticle zone

Nanocomposites

Other materials can be added to plastics to make **nanocomposite** materials. In comparison to plastics, nanocomposites can be...

- stronger
- stiffer
- lighter.

The characteristics of nanocomposites can be seen by looking at the nanostructures formed by the nanoparticles.

Key Words

Covalent bond • Nanoscience • Smart material

Nanocomposites are already being used or developed for many industries, for example...

- the car industry
- medical and dental applications
- new computers
- highly selective sensors
- new coatings and sunscreens
- stronger and lighter construction materials
- product-specific catalysts.

Smart materials are a type of nanostructure that can be designed to...

- have specific properties on a nanoscopic scale
- behave in a certain way when subjected to certain conditions.

The Periodic Table & Atoms

The Periodic Table

1	2											3	4	5	6	7	0
						1 H hydrogen 1											4 He helium 2
7 Li lithium 3	9 Be beryllium 4											11 B boron 5	12 C carbon 6	14 N nitrogen 7	16 O oxygen 8	19 F fluorine 9	20 Ne neon 10
23 Na sodium 11	24 Mg magnesium 12											27 Al aluminium 13	28 Si silicon 14	31 P phosphorus 15	32 S sulfur 16	35.5 Cl chlorine 17	40 Ar argon 18
39 K potassium 19	40 Ca calcium 20	45 Sc scandium 21	48 Ti titanium 22	51 V vanadium 23	52 Cr chromium 24	55 Mn manganese 25	56 Fe iron 26	59 Co cobalt 27	59 Ni nickel 28	63.5 Cu copper 29	65 Zn zinc 30	70 Ga gallium 31	73 Ge germanium 32	75 As arsenic 33	79 Se selenium 34	80 Br bromine 35	84 Kr krypton 36
85 Rb rubidium 37	88 Sr strontium 38	89 Y yttrium 39	91 Zr zirconium 40	93 Nb niobium 41	96 Mo molybdenum 42	[98] Tc technetium 43	101 Ru ruthenium 44	103 Rh rhodium 45	106 Pd palladium 46	108 Ag silver 47	112 Cd cadmium 48	115 In indium 49	119 Sn tin 50	122 Sb antimony 51	128 Te tellurium 52	127 I iodine 53	131 Xe xenon 54
133 Cs caesium 55	137 Ba barium 56	139 La* lanthanum 57	178 Hf hafnium 72	181 Ta tantalum 73	184 W tungsten 74	186 Re rhenium 75	190 Os osmium 76	192 Ir iridium 77	195 Pt platinum 78	197 Au gold 79	201 Hg mercury 80	204 Tl thallium 81	207 Pb lead 82	209 Bi bismuth 83	[209] Po polonium 84	[210] At astatine 85	[222] Rn radon 86
[223] Fr francium 87	[226] Ra radium 88	[227] Ac* actinium 89	[261] Rf rutherfordium 104	[262] Db dubnium 105	[266] Sg seaborgium 106	[264] Bh bohrium 107	[277] Hs hassium 108	[268] Mt meitnerium 109	[271] Ds darmstadtium 110	[272] Rg roentgenium 111							

N.B. The exact position of mass number, element name and atomic number may differ depending on the version of periodic table. However, the mass number will always be the top number, and the atomic number the bottom number.

Mass Number and Atomic Number

Atoms of an element can be described using their mass and atomic number.

The **mass number** is the total number of **protons** and **neutrons** in the atom.

The **atomic (proton) number** is the number of protons in the atom.

Mass number → 23

Atomic number → 11

$^{23}_{11}\mathrm{Na}$ ← Element symbol

Number of neutrons = Mass number − Atomic number

The number of **protons** in an atom is **equal** to the number of **electrons**. So, an atom has **no overall charge**.

1 Hydrogen

$^{1}_{1}\mathrm{H}$

1 proton

1 electron

2 Oxygen

$^{16}_{8}\mathrm{O}$

8 protons

8 electrons

Although they have the same charge, protons and electrons have a **different mass**.

Atomic Particle	Relative Mass
Proton	1
Neutron	1
Electron	Very small (negligible)

Isotopes & Relative Formula Mass

Isotopes

All atoms of a **particular element** have the **same number** of protons. Atoms of **different elements** have **different numbers** of protons.

Isotopes are atoms of the **same element** which have **different numbers of neutrons**.

Isotopes have the **same atomic number** but a **different mass number**.

For example, chlorine has two isotopes:

1. **Chlorine**

$^{35}_{17}Cl$

17 protons
17 electrons
18 neutrons (35 – 17)

2. **Chlorine**

$^{37}_{17}Cl$

17 protons
17 electrons
20 neutrons (37 – 17)

Relative Atomic Mass, A_r

The relative atomic mass (A_r) of an element is the same as its mass number.

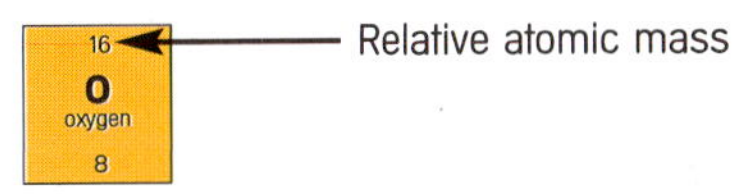

HT The **relative atomic mass, A_r** is the mass of a particular atom compared with a twelfth of the mass of a carbon atom (the ^{12}C isotope).

The A_r is an **average** value for all the **isotopes** of the element.

The **mass number** of the element is the same as the A_r of the element.

By looking at the periodic table, you can see that...
- carbon is 12 times heavier than hydrogen, but is only half as heavy as magnesium
- magnesium is three quarters as heavy as sulfur
- sulfur is twice as heavy as oxygen, etc.

You can use this idea to calculate the relative formula mass of compounds.

Relative Formula Mass, M_r

The **relative formula mass**, **M_r**, of a compound is the relative atomic masses of all its elements added together.

To calculate M_r, you need to know...
- the formula of the compound
- the A_r of all the atoms involved.

Example 1

Calculate the M_r of water, H_2O.

Write the formula → H_2O

Substitute the A_rs → $(2 \times 1) + 16$

Calculate the M_r → $2 + 16 = 18$

Example 2

Calculate the M_r of potassium carbonate, K_2CO_3.

Write the formula → K_2CO_3

Substitute the A_rs → $(39 \times 2) + 12 + (16 \times 3)$

Calculate the M_r → $78 + 12 + 48 = 138$

Key Words

Atomic number • Electron • Isotope • Mass number • Neutron • Proton • Relative atomic mass • Relative formula mass

Percentage Mass

Calculating Percentage Mass

The mass of the compound is its **relative formula mass**.

To calculate the **percentage mass** of an element in a compound, you need to know...

- the **formula** of the compound
- the **relative atomic mass** of all the atoms.

You can calculate the percentage mass by using this formula...

$$\frac{\textbf{Relative mass of element in the compound}}{\textbf{Relative formula mass of compound } (M_r)} \times 100$$

Example 1

Calculate the percentage mass of magnesium in magnesium oxide, MgO.

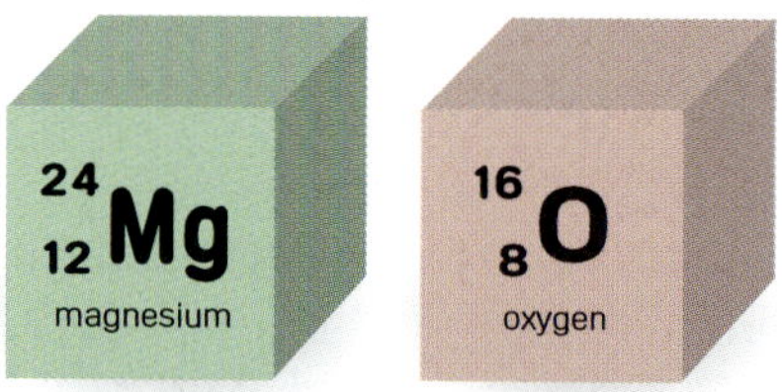

Relative mass of magnesium = 24

Relative formula mass (M_r) of MgO =

24 + 16 = 40

(A_r Mg) (A_r O) (A_r MgO)

$$\frac{\text{Relative mass of element}}{M_r \text{ of compound}} \times 100$$

$= \frac{24}{40} \times 100 =$ **60%**

Example 2

Calculate the percentage mass of potassium in potassium carbonate, K_2CO_3.

Relative mass of potassium = 39 x 2

Relative formula mass (M_r) of K_2CO_3 =

78 + 12 + 48 = 138

(A_r K x 2) (A_r C) (A_r O x 3) (A_r K_2CO_3)

$$\frac{\text{Relative mass of element}}{M_r \text{ of compound}} \times 100$$

$= \frac{78}{138} \times 100 =$ **56.5%**

HT Empirical Formula of a Compound

The empirical formula of a compound is the **simplest formula** that represents the **composition** of the compound **by mass.**

Example

Find the simplest formula of an oxide of iron produced by reacting 1.12g of iron with 0.48g of oxygen (A_r Fe = 56, A_r O = 16).

Identify the mass of the elements in the compound

Masses: Fe = 1.12, O = 0.48

Divide these masses by their relative atomic masses

$\text{Fe} = \frac{1.12}{56} = 0.02 \qquad \text{O} = \frac{0.48}{16} = 0.03$

Identify the ratio of atoms in the compound

Ratio = 0.02 : 0.03 (x 100) → 2 : 3

Empirical formula = $\mathbf{Fe_2O_3}$

The Mole

A **mole** (mol) is a measure of the **number of particles** (atoms or molecules) contained in a substance.

One mole of **any substance** (element or compound) will always contain the **same number** of particles – six hundred thousand billion billion or 6×10^{23}. This is the **relative formula mass** of the substance.

If a substance is an **element**, the mass of one mole of the substance, called the molar mass (g/mol), is always **equal** to the **relative atomic mass** of the substance in grams. For example...

Hydrogen	1 g/mol
Carbon	12 g/mol
Oxygen	16 g/mol
Sodium	23 g/mol
Magnesium	24 g/mol
Sulfur	32 g/mol
Potassium	39 g/mol

If a substance is a **compound**, the mass of one mole of the substance is always **equal** to the **relative formula mass** of the substance in grams. For example, one mole of sodium hydroxide (NaOH)...

A_r sodium + A_r hydrogen + A_r oxygen

= 23 + 1 + 16 = **40g**

You can calculate the number of moles in a substance using this formula:

$$\text{Number of moles of substance (mol)} = \frac{\text{Mass of substance (g)}}{\text{Mass of one mole (g/mol)}}$$

N.B. You need to remember this equation as it will not be given to you in the exam.

Example 1

Calculate the number of moles of carbon in 36g of the element.

$$\text{Number of moles of substance (mol)} = \frac{\text{Mass of substance (g)}}{\text{Mass of one mole (g/mol)}}$$

$$= \frac{36\text{g}}{12\text{g/mol}}$$

(A_r carbon = 12)

= **3 moles**

Example 2

Calculate the number of moles of carbon dioxide in 33g of the gas.

$$\text{Number of moles of substance (mol)} = \frac{\text{Mass of substance (g)}}{\text{Mass of one mole (g/mol)}}$$

$$= \frac{33\text{g}}{44\text{g/mol}}$$

(A_r carbon dioxide = A_r carbon + 2 x A_r oxygen = 12 + (2 x 16) = 44)

= **0.75 mole**

Example 3

Calculate the mass of 4 moles of sodium hydroxide.

Rearrange the formula...

$$\text{Mass of substance (g)} = \text{Number of moles of substance (mol)} \times \text{Mass of one mole (g/mol)}$$

= 4mol x 40g/mol

= **160g**

N.B. If you are confident in your mathematical ability, you can also do these calculations using ratios.

Key Words

Mole • Relative atomic mass • Relative formula mass

Calculating Mass

HT Calculating the Mass of a Product

Example

Calculate how much calcium oxide can be produced from 50kg of calcium carbonate.
(Relative atomic masses: Ca = 40, C = 12, O = 16).

1. Write down the equation.
2. Work out the M_r of each substance.
3. Check that the total mass of reactants equals the total mass of the products. If they are not the same, check your work.
4. The question only mentions calcium oxide and calcium carbonate, so you can now ignore the carbon dioxide. You just need the ratio of mass of reactant to mass of product.
5. Use the ratio to calculate how much calcium oxide can be produced.

1. $CaCO_3 \rightarrow CaO + CO_2$
2. $40 + 12 + (3 \times 16) \rightarrow (40 + 16) + [12 + (2 \times 16)]$
3. $100 \rightarrow 56 + 44$ ✔
4. 100 : 56
5. If 100kg of $CaCO_3$ produces 56kg of CaO,
then 1kg of $CaCO_3$ produces $\frac{56}{100}$kg of CaO,
and 50kg of $CaCO_3$ produces $\frac{56}{100} \times 50$
= **28kg of CaO.**

Calculating the Mass of a Reactant

Example

Calculate how much aluminium oxide is needed to produce 540 tonnes of aluminium.
(Relative atomic masses: Al = 27, O = 16).

1. Write down the equation.
2. Work out the M_r of each substance.
3. Check that the total mass of reactants equals the total mass of the products. If they are not the same, check your work.
4. The question only mentions aluminium oxide and aluminium, so you can now ignore the oxygen. You just need the ratio of mass of reactant to mass of product.
5. Use the ratio to calculate how much aluminium oxide is needed.

1. $2Al_2O_3 \rightarrow 4Al + 3O_2$
2. $2 \times [(2 \times 27) + (3 \times 16)] \rightarrow (4 \times 27) + [3 \times (2 \times 16)]$
3. $204 \rightarrow 108 + 96$ ✔
4. 204 : 108
5. If 204 tonnes of Al_2O_3 produces 108 tonnes of Al,
then $\frac{204}{108}$ tonnes is needed to produce 1 tonne of Al,
and $\frac{204}{108} \times 540$ tonnes is needed to produce 540 tonnes of Al
= **1020 tonnes of Al_2O_3.**

Yield & Atom Economy

Yield

Atoms are **never lost or gained** in a chemical reaction. But, it isn't always possible to obtain the calculated amount of the product because...

- if the reaction is reversible, it might not go to completion
- some product could be lost when it is separated from the reaction mixture
- some of the reactants may react in different ways to the expected reaction.

HT The amount of product obtained is called the **yield**.

The **percentage yield** can be calculated by comparing...

- the actual yield obtained from a reaction
- the maximum theoretical yield.

$$\text{Percentage yield} = \frac{\text{Yield from reaction}}{\text{Maximum theoretical yield}} \times 100$$

Example

50kg of calcium carbonate ($CaCO_3$) is expected to produce 28kg of calcium oxide (CaO).

A company heats 50kg of calcium carbonate in a kiln and obtains 22kg of calcium oxide.

Calculate the percentage yield.

$$\text{Percentage yield} = \frac{22}{28} \times 100 = \mathbf{78.6\%}$$

Calculating Atom Economy

Chemical reactions often produce more than one **product**. However, not all of these products are **'useful'**. A useful product is one that can be used in industry.

Atom economy (atom utilisation) is a measure of the **amount of starting materials** (reactants) that end up as **useful products**.

$$\text{Atom economy} = \frac{M_r \text{ of useful products}}{M_r \text{ of reactants}} \times 100$$

In industry, it's important to use reactions which have a **high atom economy** in order to...

- make the reaction economical
- ensure sustainable development.

Example

Calcium carbonate → Calcium oxide + Carbon dioxide

The products of this reaction are calcium oxide (useful) and carbon dioxide (waste).

Calculate the atom economy of this reaction.

1. Calculate the M_r of the reactants and products

$$CaCO_3 \rightarrow CaO + CO_2$$

M_r of $CaCO_3$ = 40 + 12 + (3 x 16) = **100**

M_r of CaO = 40 + 16 = **56**

M_r of CO_2 = 12 + (2 x 16) = **44**

2. Calculate the atom economy

$$\text{Atom economy} = \frac{56}{100} \times 100 = \mathbf{56\%}$$

Key Words

Atom economy • Yield

Reversible Reactions & the Haber Process

Reversible Reactions

Some chemical reactions are **reversible**. In a **reversible reaction**, the **products** can **react** to produce the **original reactants**.

These reactions are represented as...

$$A + B \rightleftharpoons C + D$$

This means that A and B can react to produce C and D, and C and D can also react to produce A and B.

For example...

Ammonium chloride	$\rightleftharpoons$	Ammonia	+	Hydrogen chloride
NH_4Cl	$\rightleftharpoons$	NH_3	+	HCl

Solid ammonium chloride decomposes when heated to produce ammonia and hydrogen chloride gas (both colourless).

Ammonia reacts with hydrogen chloride gas to produce clouds of white ammonium chloride powder.

The Haber Process

Reversible reactions may not go to completion. However, they can still be used efficiently in continuous processes such as the **Haber Process.**

The Haber process is used to manufacture **ammonia**. The raw materials for this process are...

- **nitrogen** – from the fractional distillation of liquid air
- **hydrogen** – from natural gas and steam.

The purified nitrogen and hydrogen are passed over an **iron catalyst** at a...

- **high temperature** (about 450 C)
- **high pressure** (about 200 atmospheres).

Some of the hydrogen and nitrogen **reacts** to **form ammonia**.

The **ammonia** produced can **break down** again into **nitrogen** and **hydrogen**.

Nitrogen	+	Hydrogen	$\rightleftharpoons$	Ammonia
N_2	+	$3H_2$	$\rightleftharpoons$	$2NH_3$

HT These reaction conditions are chosen to produce a **reasonable yield** of ammonia quickly.

Even so, only **some** of the hydrogen and nitrogen react together to form ammonia.

The Haber Process

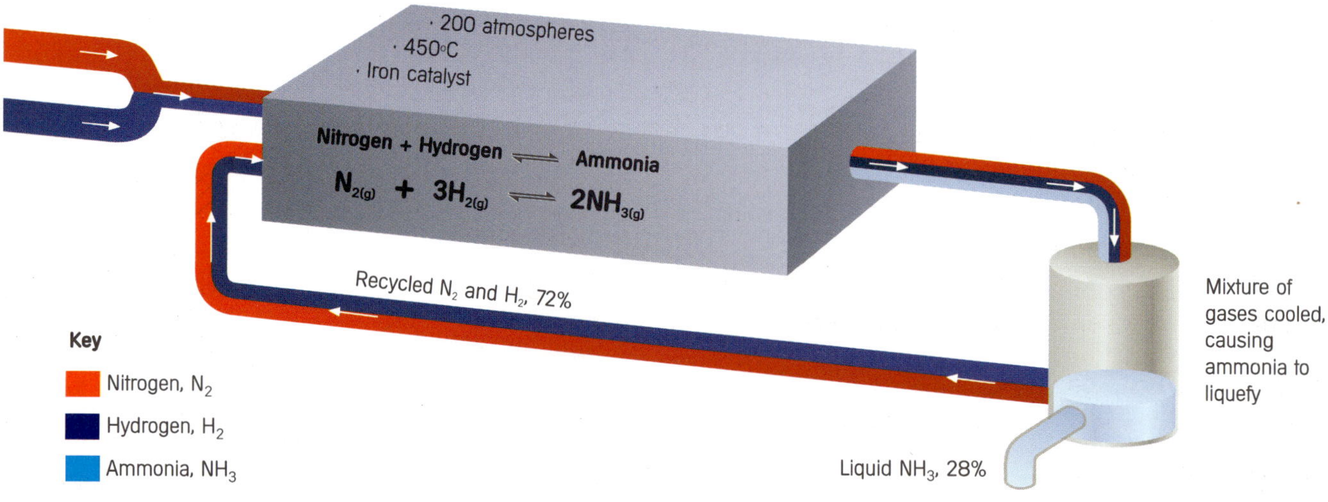

Rates of Reactions

Chemical reactions only occur when reacting particles **collide** with each other with **sufficient energy**.

The **minimum amount** of energy required to cause a reaction is called the **activation energy**.

There are four important factors which affect the rate of reaction:

- Temperature.
- Concentration.
- Surface area.
- Use of a catalyst.

Temperature

In a **cold** reaction mixture, the particles move quite **slowly**. They collide less often, with less energy, so **fewer collisions** are successful.

In a **hot** reaction mixture the particles move more **quickly**. They collide more often, with greater energy, so **more collisions** are successful.

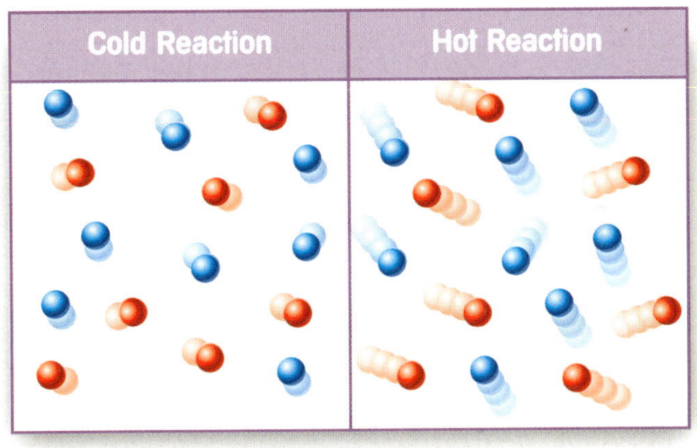

Concentration

In a **low concentration** reaction, the particles are **spread out**. They collide less often, so there are fewer successful collisions.

In a **high concentration** reaction, the particles are crowded **close together**. They collide more often, so there are more successful collisions.

Increasing the **pressure** of reacting gases also increases the frequency of collisions.

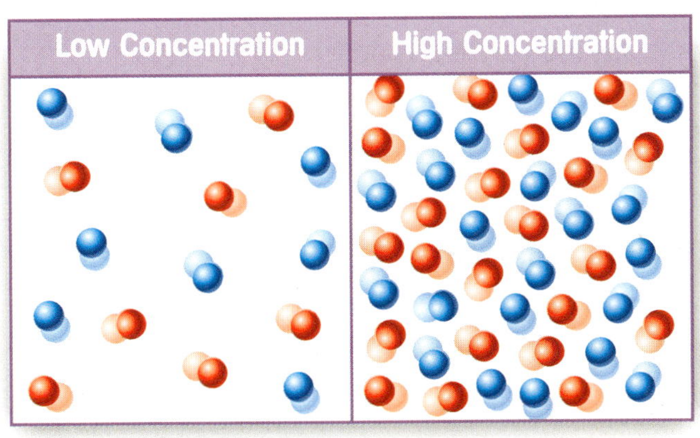

Increase in pressure increases rate of reaction

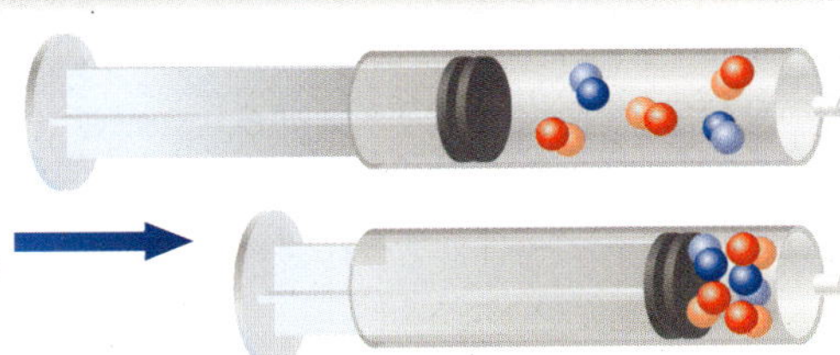

HT **Concentrations** of solutions are given in **moles per cubic decimetre (mol/dm^3)**.

Equal volumes of solutions of the same molar concentration contain the same number of moles of solute, i.e. the same number of particles.

Equal volumes of gases at the same temperature and pressure contain the **same number** of molecules.

Key Words

Activation energy • Catalyst • Reversible reaction • Yield

Chemical Reactions

Surface Area

Large pieces of a solid reactant have a **small surface area** in relation to their volume.

Fewer particles are exposed and available for collisions. This means **fewer collisions** and a **slower reaction**.

Small pieces of a solid reactant have a **large surface area** in relation to their volume, so more particles are exposed and available for collisions.

This means **more collisions** and a **faster reaction**.

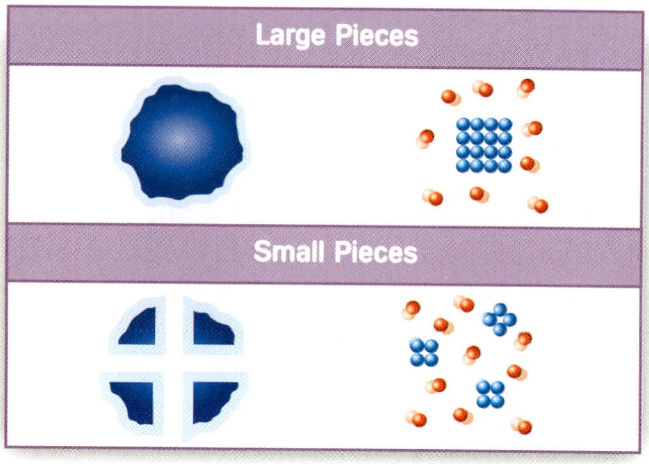

Using a Catalyst

A **catalyst** is a substance which **increases the rate** of a chemical reaction without being used up or altered in the process.

A catalyst...

- reduces the amount of energy needed for a successful collision
- makes more collisions successful
- speeds up the reaction
- provides a surface for the molecules to attach to, which increases their chances of bumping into each other.

Different reactions need different catalysts, e.g....

- the cracking of hydrocarbons uses broken pottery
- the manufacture of ammonia uses iron.

Increasing the rates of chemical reactions is important in industry because it helps to **reduce costs**.

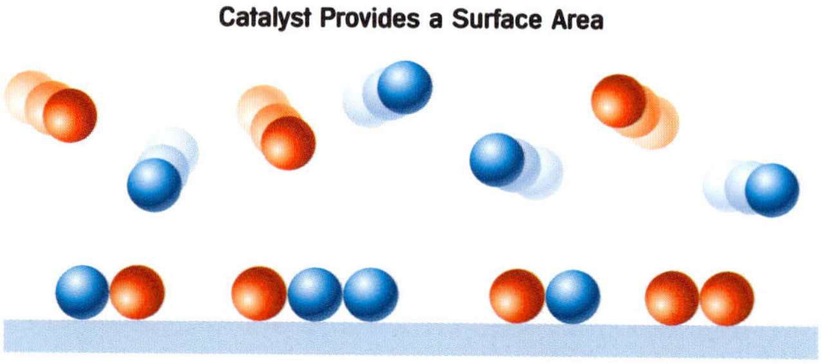

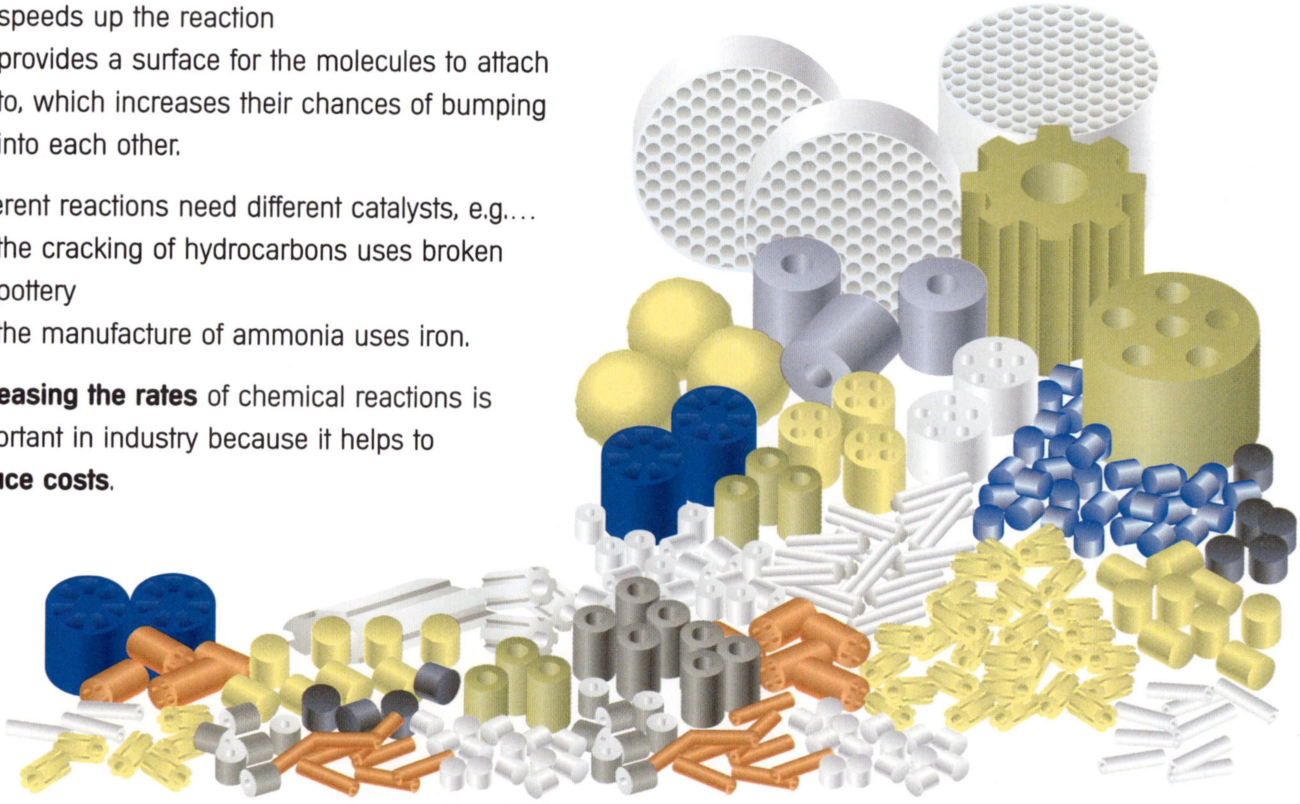

Analysing the Rate of Reaction

$$\text{Rate of Reaction} = \frac{\text{Amount of reactant used / product formed}}{\text{Time}}$$

The rate of a chemical reaction can be found by:

1. **Measuring the amount of reactants used.** If one of the products is a gas, you could weigh the reaction mixture before and after the reaction takes place. The mass of the mixture will decrease.

2. **Measuring the amount of products formed.** You could use a gas syringe to measure the total volume of gas produced at timed intervals.

Plotting Reaction Rates

Graphs can be plotted to show the progress of a chemical reaction. There are three things to remember:

1. The steeper the line, the faster the reaction.
2. When one of the reactants is used up, the reaction stops (lines become horizontal).
3. The same amount of product is formed from the same amount of reactants, irrespective of rate.

The graph shows us that reaction **A** is faster than reaction **B**. This could be because...

- the surface area of the solid reactants in **A** is greater than in **B**
- the temperature of reaction **A** is greater than reaction **B**
- the concentration of the solution in **A** is greater than in **B**
- a catalyst is used in reaction **A** but not in reaction **B**.

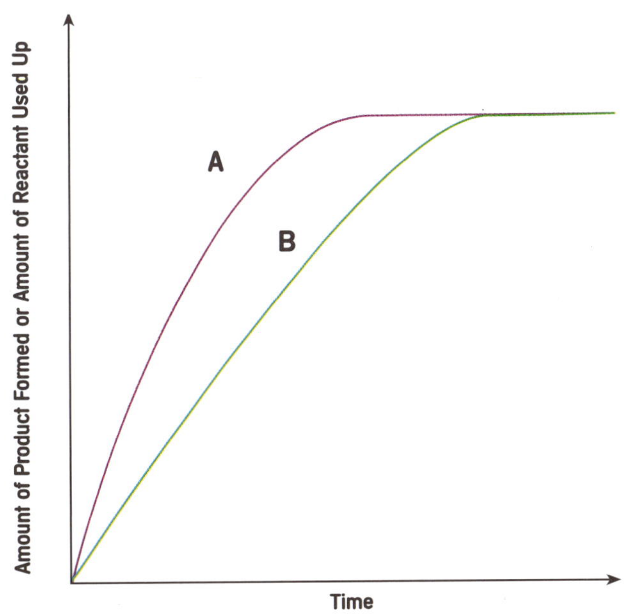

Key Word

Catalyst

Exothermic & Endothermic Reactions

Chemical Reactions

When chemical reactions occur, **energy** is transferred **to** or **from** the **surroundings**.

Many chemical reactions are, therefore, accompanied by a **temperature change**.

Exothermic Reactions

Exothermic reactions are accompanied by a **temperature rise**. They transfer heat energy to the surroundings, i.e. they **give out** heat.

Common examples of exothermic reactions include...

- neutralising alkalis with acids
- oxidation
- combustion.

Methane (natural gas)	+	Oxygen	→	Carbon dioxide	+	Water	+	Heat energy
CH_4	+	$2O_2$	→	CO_2	+	$2H_2O$		

Carbon	+	Oxygen	→	Carbon dioxide	+	Heat energy
C	+	O_2	→	CO_2		

Endothermic Reactions

Endothermic reactions are accompanied by a **fall in temperature**. Heat energy is transferred from the surroundings, i.e. they **take in** heat.

Thermal decomposition and dissolving ammonium nitrate crystals in water are examples of endothermic reactions.

Ammonium nitrate	+	Water	→	Ammonium nitrate solution	–	Heat energy
NH_4NO_3	+	H_2O	→	NH_4NO_3		

HT Changing Reaction Conditions

In an **exothermic** reaction...

- if the temperature is **raised**, the yield **decreases**
- if the temperature is **lowered**, the yield **increases**.

In an **endothermic** reaction...

- if the temperature is **raised**, the yield **increases**
- if the temperature is **lowered**, the yield **decreases**.

In **gaseous reactions,** an increase in pressure favours the reaction which produces the least number of molecules.

These factors, together with reaction rates, determine the optimum conditions in industrial processes, e.g. the **Haber process**.

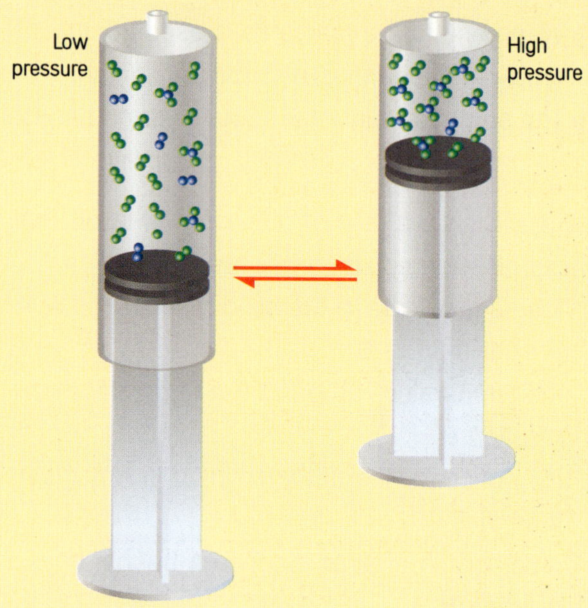

Reversible Reactions

If a reversible reaction is **exothermic in one direction**, then it follows that it is **endothermic in the opposite direction**. The **same amount of energy** is transferred in each case.

An example of this is when hydrated copper sulfate is gently heated.

Hydrated copper sulfate (blue)	+	Heat energy	$\rightleftharpoons$	Anhydrous copper sulfate (white)	+	Water
$CuSO_4.5H_2O$			$\rightleftharpoons$	$CuSO_4$	+	$5H_2O$

Hydrated Copper Sulfate

Anhydrous Copper Sulfate

Water Being Added to Anhydrous Copper Sulfate

If water is added to white anhydrous copper sulfate, heat is given out and blue hydrated copper sulfate is formed.

The blue crystals of hydrated copper sulfate can then be heated. Heat is taken in, the water is removed, and white anhydrous copper sulfate is formed.

This reverse reaction can be used as a test for the presence of water. If the copper sulfate changes from white to blue then water is present.

Sustainable Development

It is important to minimise energy use and wastage in industrial processes for...
- sustainable development
- economic reasons.

Non-vigorous conditions mean...
- less energy is used
- less energy is released into the environment
- a less efficient reaction.

In an **industrial process production**...
- an **efficient** reaction takes place in a short time, so less energy is needed or wasted, and the cost is reduced
- an **inefficient** reaction takes a long time, so more energy is needed and wasted, so more energy is used.

Key Words

Endothermic • Exothermic • Reversible reaction • Yield

Reversible Reactions & Closed Systems

HT Reversible Reactions

The manufacture of ammonia in the **Haber process** is a **reversible reaction**. It involves energy transfers associated with the **breaking** and **forming** of chemical bonds.

$$N_2 + 3H_2 \underset{\text{Endothermic}}{\overset{\text{Exothermic}}{\rightleftharpoons}} 2NH_3$$

The **volume** of ammonia produced is **less** than the total volume of the **reactants** (nitrogen and hydrogen).

Less energy is needed to **break the bonds** between the nitrogen and hydrogen molecules than is **released** in the **formation** of the ammonia molecules.

Altering the **temperature** and **pressure** can have a big impact on the production of ammonia:

- **High pressure** produces a high yield at a fast rate, but it's very expensive.
- **Low pressure** is less expensive, but produces a low yield at a slow rate.
- **Low temperature** produces a high yield but the reaction is very slow.
- **High temperature** leads to a fast reaction, but a low yield is produced.

The conditions have to be chosen very carefully so that they are economically viable **and** can meet demand. So, a compromise solution is reached:

- Pressure = 200 atmospheres.
- Temperature = 450°C.

Closed Systems

In a **closed system**, no reactants are added and no products are removed.

When a reversible reaction occurs in a closed system, an **equilibrium** is achieved when the reactions occur at exactly the **same rate** in **each direction**.

The relative amounts of all the reacting substances at equilibrium depend on the conditions of the reaction.

Look at this reaction:

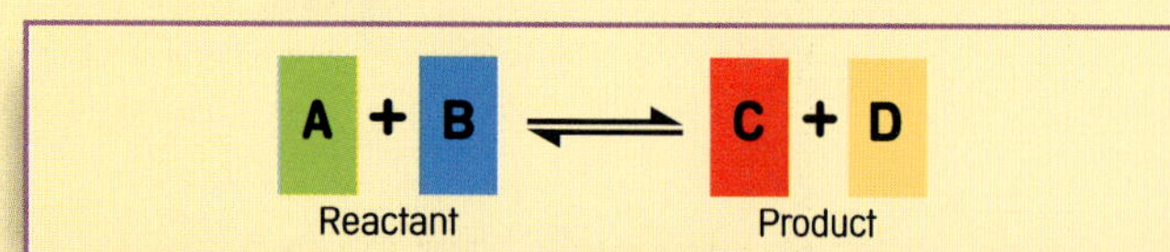

If the forward reaction (the reaction that produces the products C and D) is **endothermic** then...

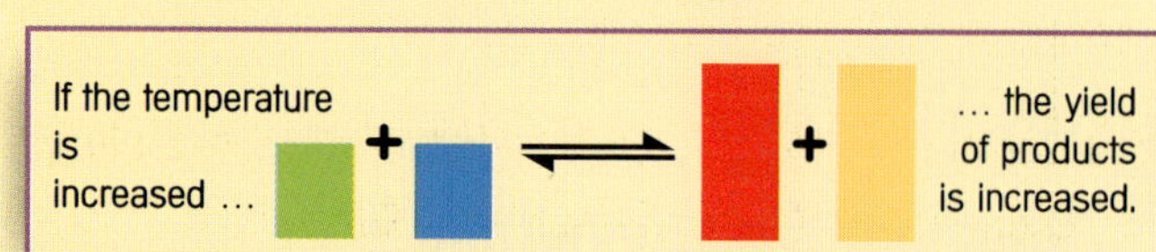

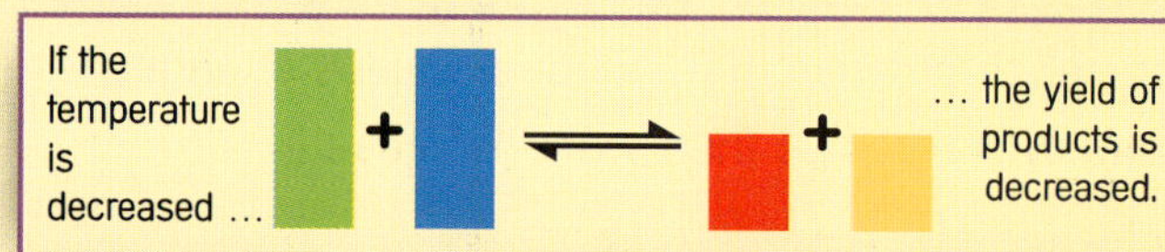

If the forward reaction is **exothermic** then...

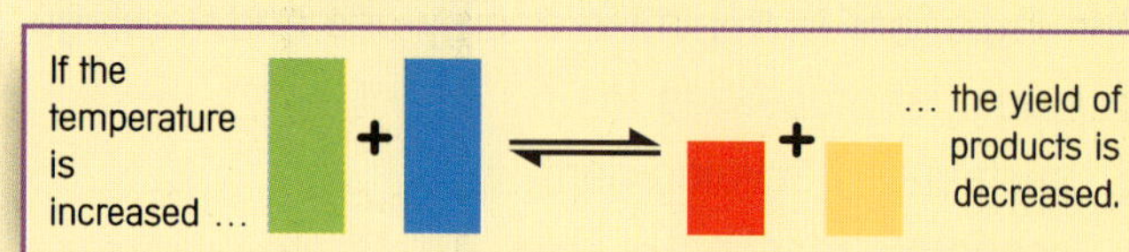

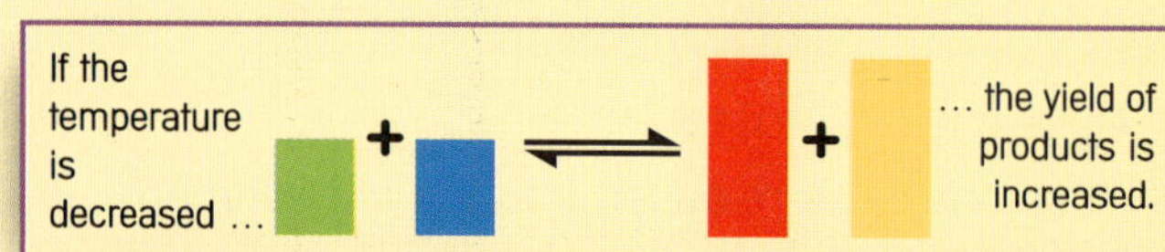

Even though a reversible reaction may not go to completion, it may still be used efficiently in an industrial process.

State Symbols

State symbols are used in equations. The symbols are **(s) solid, (l) liquid, (g) gas** and **(aq) aqueous**.

An **aqueous solution** is produced when a substance is **dissolved in water**.

Electrolysis

Electrolysis is the **breaking down** of a compound containing **ions**, into its **elements** using an **electrical current**.

Ionic substances are chemical compounds that allow an **electric current** to flow through them when they are...

- molten
- dissolved in water.

These compounds contain **negative** and **positive** ions. During electrolysis...

- **negatively charged ions** move to the **positive electrode**
- **positively charged ions** move to the **negative electrode**.

When this happens, simpler substances are released at the two electrodes.

This moving of electrons forms electrically **neutral** atoms or molecules which are then released.

If there is a **mixture of ions** in the solution, the products formed depend on the reactivity of the elements involved.

For example, in the electrolysis of **copper chloride solution**, the simple substances released are...

- copper at the negative electrode
- chlorine gas at the positive electrode.

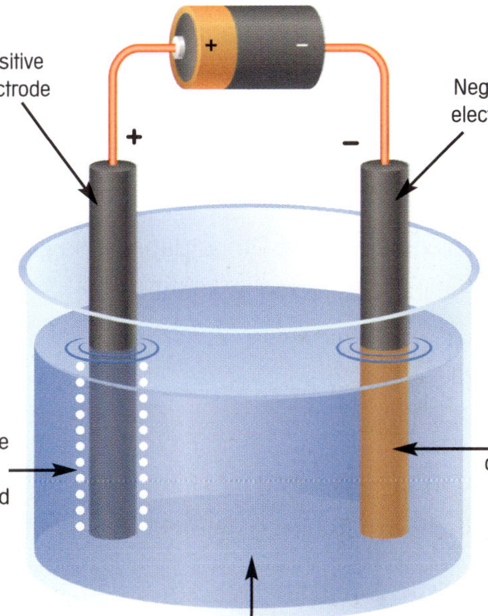

Redox Reactions

Reduction is when **positively** charged ions **gain** electrons at the **negative** electrode.

Key Words

Current • Electrode • Electrolysis • Equilibrium • Ion • Oxidation • Reduction

Oxidation is when **negatively** charged ions **lose** electrons at the **positive** electrode.

A **redox** reaction is a chemical reaction where **both reduction** and **oxidation** occur.

You can remember this by thinking of the word **oilrig**:

- **O**xidation **I**s **L**oss of electrons (**OIL**)
- **R**eduction **I**s **G**ain of electrons (**RIG**)

Electrolysis

Electrolysis of Sodium Chloride Solution

Sodium chloride (common salt) is a compound of an alkali metal and a halogen. It is found in large quantities in the sea and in underground deposits.

Electrolysis of sodium chloride solution (brine) produces some important reagents for the chemical industry...

- **chlorine gas** (at the positive **electrode**)
- **hydrogen gas** (at the negative electrode)
- **sodium hydroxide solution** (passed out of the cell).

Chlorine is used to kill bacteria in drinking water and swimming pools, and to manufacture hydrochloric acid, disinfectants, bleach and PVC.

Hydrogen is used in the manufacture of ammonia and margarine.

Sodium hydroxide is used in the manufacture of soap, paper and ceramics.

Chlorine bleaches damp litmus paper. This is how its presence can be detected in a laboratory.

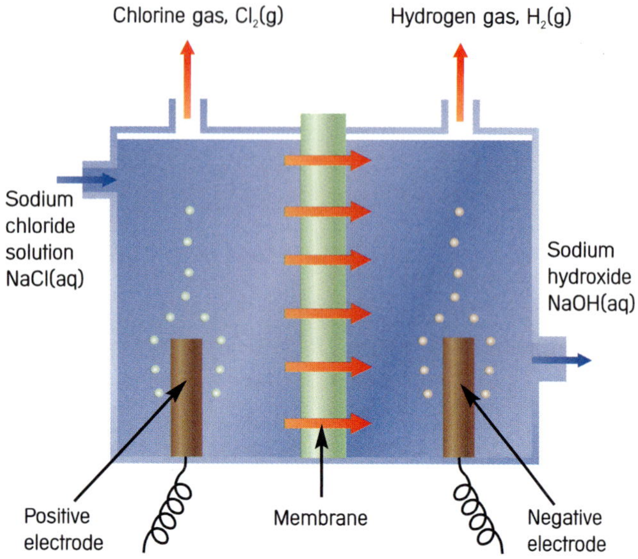

Sodium chloride + **Water** $\xrightarrow{\text{electrolysis}}$ **Hydrogen** + **Chlorine** + **Sodium hydroxide**

$$2NaCl(aq) + 2H_2O(l) \rightarrow H_2(g) + Cl_2(g) + 2NaOH(aq)$$

Purification of Copper by Electrolysis

Copper can be **extracted by reduction**, but when it is needed in a pure form it is **purified by electrolysis**.

For electrolysis to take place...

- the positive electrode needs to be made of impure copper
- the negative electrode needs to be made of pure copper
- the solution must contain copper ions.

When an electrical current is passed into the solution, copper **ions** from the **positive electrode** pass into the solution and move towards the negative electrode.

At the **negative electrode**, the copper ions become **copper atoms** which stick to the pure copper electrode.

So, the negative electrode gets bigger, whilst the positive electrode seems to dissolve away and the impurities fall to the bottom of the solution.

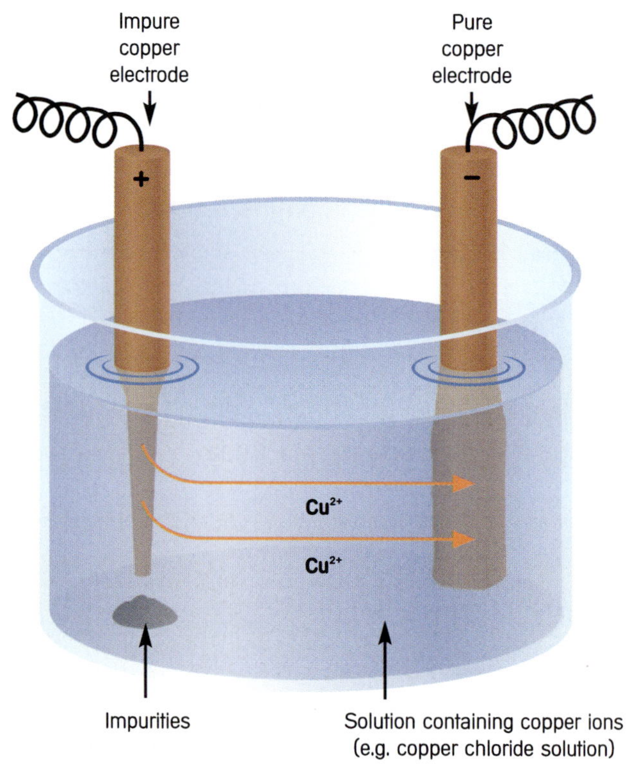

HT Electrolysis Equations

Reactions that occur at the electrodes during electrolysis can be represented by **half-equations**.

For example, in the electrolysis of copper...

- copper is deposited at the **negative electrode**

$$Cu^{2+} + 2e^{-} \longrightarrow Cu(s)$$

- chlorine gas is given off at the **positive electrode**. (Remember that chlorine exists as molecules.)

$$2Cl^{-} - 2e^{-} \longrightarrow Cl_2(g)$$

N.B. When writing equations, remember to include the state symbols.

Indicators and pH Scale

Indicators are dyes which change colour depending on whether they are in **acidic** or **alkaline** solutions:

- **Litmus** is an indicator which changes colour from red to blue or vice versa.
- **Universal indicator** is a mixture of dyes which show a **range** of colours to indicate **how** acidic or alkaline a substance is.

The **pH scale** is a measure of the **acidity or alkalinity** of an **aqueous solution**, across a **14-point scale**. When substances dissolve in water, they dissociate into their individual ions:

- Hydroxide ions, $OH^{-}(aq)$, make solutions alkaline.
- Hydrogen ions, $H^{+}(aq)$, make solutions acidic.

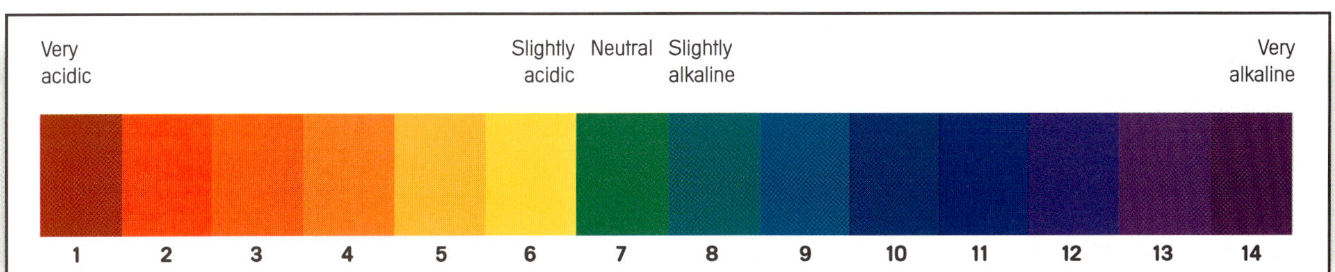

Key Words

Acid • Alkali • Electrode • Electrolysis • Ion • pH • Reduction

Neutralisation

Neutralisation

Acids and **alkalis** are **chemical opposites**:

- **Acids** contain **hydrogen ions**, $H^+(aq)$.
- **Alkalis** contain **hydroxide ions**, $OH^-(aq)$.

If they are added together in the correct amounts they can 'cancel out' each other.

When an acid reacts with an alkali, the **ions** react together to produce **water** (pH 7).

$$H^+(aq) + OH^-(aq) \longrightarrow H_2O(l)$$

This type of reaction is called **neutralisation** because the solution that remains has a pH of 7, showing it is neutral. For example, hydrochloric acid and potassium hydroxide can be neutralised.

Hydrochloric acid	+	Potassium hydroxide	⟶	Potassium chloride	+	Water
$HCl(l)$	+	$KOH(l)$	⟶	$KCl(s)$	+	$H_2O(l)$

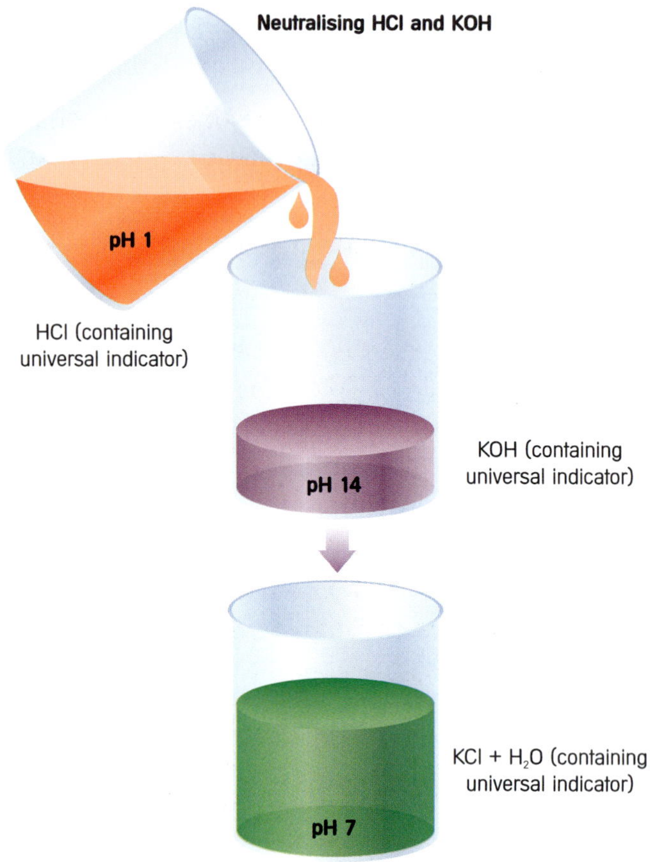

Neutralising Ammonia

Ammonia is an **alkaline gas** which dissolves in water to make an **alkaline solution**.

It is mainly used in the production of fertilisers to increase the nitrogen content of the soil.

Ammonia neutralises nitric acid to produce **ammonium nitrate**. The aqueous ammonium nitrate is then evaporated to dryness.

Ammonia	+	Nitric acid	⟶	Ammonium nitrate
$NH_3(aq)$	+	$HNO_3(aq)$	⟶	$NH_4NO_3(aq)$

Ammonium nitrate, a fertiliser rich in nitrogen, is also known as 'nitram' (nitrate of ammonia). **Nitrogen-based fertilisers** are important chemicals because they increase the yields of crops. However, nitrates can create problems if they find their way into streams, rivers or groundwater. They can...

- upset the natural balance of water
- contaminate our drinking water.

Ammonium can be neutralised with acids to produce ammonium salts.

	Hydrochloric Acid	Sulfuric Acid	Nitric Acid
Ammonium Hydroxide	Ammonium chloride and water	Ammonium sulfate and water	Ammonium nitrate and water

Key Words

Acid • Alkali • Insoluble • Ion • Neutralisation • Precipitation • Salt

Forming Salts

Soluble Salts from Metals

Metals react with dilute acid to form a **metal salt** and **hydrogen**.

Salt is a word used to describe any metal compound made from a reaction between a metal and an acid.

Metal + Acid ⟶ Salt + Hydrogen

Some metals react with acid more vigorously than others:

- Silver – no reaction.
- Zinc – fairly reasonable reaction.
- Magnesium – vigorous reaction.
- Potassium – very violent and dangerous reaction.

Soluble Salts from Insoluble Bases

Bases are the oxides and hydroxides of metals. Soluble bases are called **alkalis**.

The oxides and hydroxides of transition metals are **insoluble**. Their salts are prepared in the following way:

1. The metal oxide or hydroxide is added to an acid until no more will react.
2. The excess metal oxide or hydroxide is then filtered, leaving a solution of the salt.
3. The salt solution is then evaporated.

This reaction can be written generally as...

Acid + Base ⟶ Neutral salt solution + Water

Example

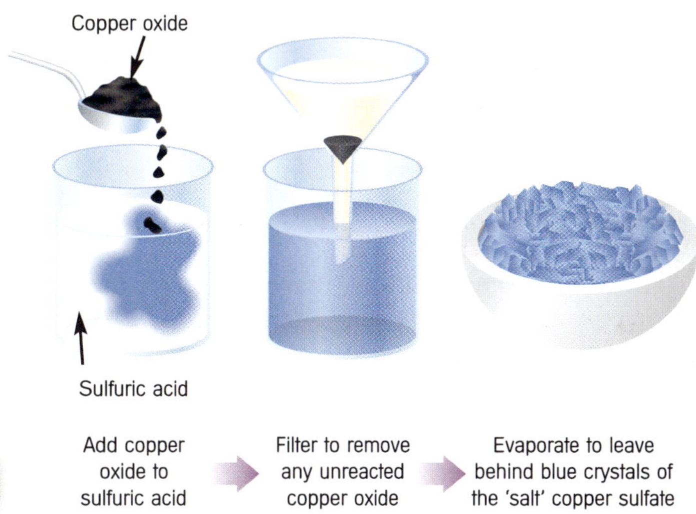

Salts of Alkali Metals

Compounds of alkali metals, called **salts**, can be made by reacting solutions of their hydroxides (which are alkaline) with a particular acid. This neutralisation reaction can be represented as follows...

Acid + Alkaline hydroxide solution ⟶ Neutral salt solution + Water

The salt produced depends on the metal in the alkali and the acid used.

	Hydrochloric Acid	Sulfuric Acid	Nitric Acid
Sodium Hydroxide	Sodium chloride and water	Sodium sulfate and water	Sodium nitrate and water
Potassium Hydroxide	Potassium chloride and water	Potassium sulfate and water	Potassium nitrate and water

Insoluble Salts

Insoluble salts can be made by mixing appropriate solutions of ions so that a precipitate (solid substance) is formed.

Precipitation can be used to remove unwanted ions from a solution, e.g. softening hard water. The calcium (or magnesium) ions are precipitated out as insoluble calcium (or magnesium) carbonate.

Chemistry Unit 2 Summary

Atoms

Nucleus = protons (positive) + neutrons (no charge).

Nucleus surrounded by electrons (negative). Atom has no overall charge.

Isotopes = atoms of the same element with different number of neutrons.

Atomic number = number of protons in an atom.

Mass number = number of protons and neutrons in an atom.

Atoms are arranged in the periodic table in **groups** and **periods**. Alkali metals = 1 electron in the outer shell. Halogens = 7 electrons in the outer shell. When atoms form chemical bonds, their outer shell of electrons changes.

HT **Relative atomic mass** (A_r) = the mass of a particular atom (compared with $\frac{1}{12}$ of the mass of a carbon atom).

Relative formula mass (M_r) = the relative atomic masses of all the elements added together.

Compound = two or more elements chemically combined together.

Mixture = two or more elements or compounds not chemically combined.

Ionic and Covalent Bonds

Ionic compounds = giant structures held together by strong forces of attraction between oppositely charged ions.

Ionic bonds → metal and non-metal atoms → electrons are transferred

Covalent bonds → non-metal atoms → electrons are shared

Giant covalent structures = strong, covalent bonds and high melting points, e.g. diamond, graphite, silicon dioxide.

HT Metals can conduct heat and electricity because they have **delocalised electrons**.

Moles

A **mole** = measure of the number of particles contained in a substance.

Element → mass of one mole = **relative atomic mass**.

Compound → mass of one mole = **relative formula mass**.

Yield and Atom Economy

Atoms are never lost or gained in a chemical reaction.

Atom economy = measure of the starting materials that end up as useful products.

HT

$$\text{Percentage yield} = \frac{\text{Yield from reaction}}{\text{Maximum theoretical yield}} \times 100$$

Chemistry Unit 2 Summary

Reversible Reactions

Reversible reaction:

$$A + B \underset{\text{endothermic}}{\overset{\text{exothermic}}{\rightleftharpoons}} C + D$$

The Haber process = nitrogen + hydrogen → ammonia

HT Both demand and economic viability have to be considered in the Haber process. A compromise of 200 atmospheres pressure and 450°C are used.

Reversible reaction occurs in a closed system → **equilibrium** achieved when the reactions occur at the same rate in the same direction.

Chemical Reactions

Activation energy = minimum amount of energy required to cause a reaction.

Reaction rates can be affected by temperature, concentration, surface area and use of a catalyst. Reaction rates can be found by measuring the amount of reactants used, or measuring the amount of products formed.

- **Exothermic** reactions **give out** heat.
- **Endothermic** reactions **take in** heat.

HT **Exothermic** reaction → raised temperatures decrease yields → lowered temperatures increase yields.

Endothermic reaction → raised temperatures increase yields → lowered temperatures decrease yields.

Electrolysis

Electrolysis = breaking down of an ionic compound into its elements using an electrical current.

Negative ions → positive electrode

Positive ions → negative electrode

Copper can be purified by electrolysis. The electrolysis of sodium chloride solution produces...

- chlorine gas at the positive electrode
- hydrogen gas at the negative electrode
- sodium hydroxide solution.

Neutralisation and Forming Salts

Acid + Alkali = neutral solutions

Metals react with dilute acid to form a metal salt and hydrogen. Compounds of alkali metals can be made by reacting solutions of their hydroxides.

Chemistry Practice Questions

1 There are four parts to this question. For each part, tick the correct answer.

The following information describes the structure of the sodium atom. Use this information to answer the questions that follow.

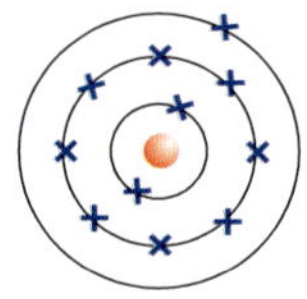

$^{23}_{11}Na$

a) Which subatomic particle does + represent?

- **i)** Electron ☐
- **ii)** Neutron ☐
- **iii)** Proton ☐
- **iv)** Nucleus ☐

b) How many neutrons does an atom of sodium have?

- **i)** 1 ☐
- **ii)** 23 ☐
- **iii)** 11 ☐
- **iv)** 12 ☐

c) Which group of the Periodic Table does sodium belong to?

- **i)** Group 1 ☐
- **ii)** Group 4 ☐
- **iii)** Group 5 ☐
- **iv)** Group 7 ☐

d) What kind of ion will an atom of sodium produce?

- **i)** Positive ☐
- **ii)** Negative ☐
- **iii)** Neutral ☐
- **iv)** Radioactive ☐

2 Ammonia is prepared in industry by reacting the raw materials hydrogen and nitrogen. The reaction is shown as: $N_2 + 3H_2 \rightleftharpoons 2NH_3$

a) What do the arrows $\rightleftharpoons$ show about the reaction? ....

b) The reaction to make ammonia is **exothermic**. What does exothermic mean?

....

c) Give the sources of the following two reactants...

Nitrogen: .... Hydrogen: ....

d) Explain why a high pressure helps the formation of ammonia.

....

e) A catalyst is used to help the formation of ammonia.

i) What is the name of the catalyst used? ....

ii) Why is a catalyst used? ....

3 Sodium hydroxide (NaOH) is also known as caustic soda.

a) Calculate the relative formula mass (M_r) of sodium hydroxide. (A_r: Na = 23, H = 1, O = 16.)

....

b) Calculate the percentage of oxygen in sodium hydroxide.

....

c) Calculate the mass of oxygen in 5g of sodium hydroxide.

....

d) Calculate the mass of 4 moles of sodium hydroxide.

....

4 **a)** Diamond and graphite are different forms of carbon. Explain, with reference to the arrangement of carbon atoms, why diamond is a very hard substance.

....

b) Give one property of silicon dioxide that both diamond and graphite have.

....

5 The diagram shows the apparatus used for the electrolysis of copper chloride solution.

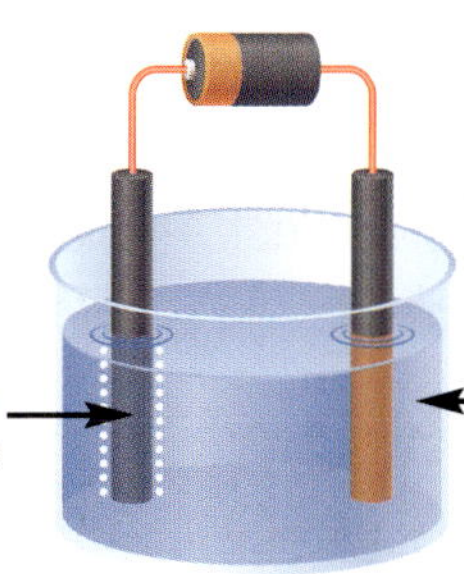

a) Name the gas produced at the positive electrode.

....

b) Why do copper ions move to the negative electrode?

....

....

c) What is the difference between reduction and oxidation in terms of electrons?

....

6 Complete the following word equations which show the formation of salts.

a) Hydrochloric acid + Potassium hydroxide ⟶ .... + Water

b) .... + Copper oxide ⟶ Copper sulfate + Water

c) Nitric acid + ... ⟶ Sodium nitrate + Water

d) Barium chloride + Zinc sulfate ⟶ .... + ...

e) What is the name of the only insoluble salt in the equations above? ....

Speed

Speed

The **speed** of an object is a measure of **how fast** it is moving.

To work out the speed of any moving object, you need to know...

- the **distance** it travels
- the **time it takes** to travel that distance.

The cyclist below travels a **distance** of 8 metres every second. So, you can say that his speed is 8 metres per second (m/s).

You can calculate speed using this formula...

$$\text{Speed (m/s)} = \frac{\text{Distance travelled (m)}}{\text{Time taken (s)}}$$

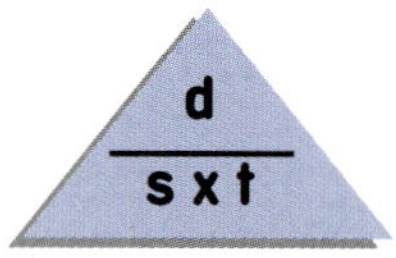

Speed can be measured in...

- metres per second (m/s)
- kilometres per hour (km/h)
- miles per hour (mph).

Distance–Time Graphs

The **slope** of a **distance–time graph** represents the **speed** of an object. The **steeper the slope**, the **greater the speed**.

The graph shows...

1. a stationary person
2. a person moving at a constant speed of 2m/s
3. a person moving at a greater constant speed of 3m/s.

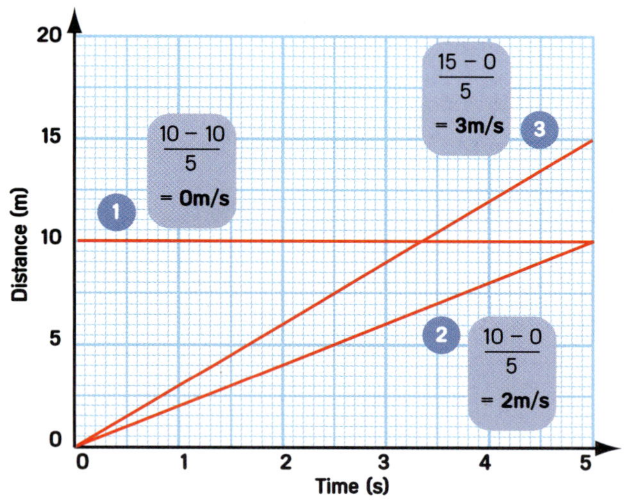

N.B. The vertical axis shows distance from a fixed point (O), not total distance travelled.

Velocity

Velocity and speed **aren't** the same thing. The velocity of a moving object describes **its speed** in a **given direction**.

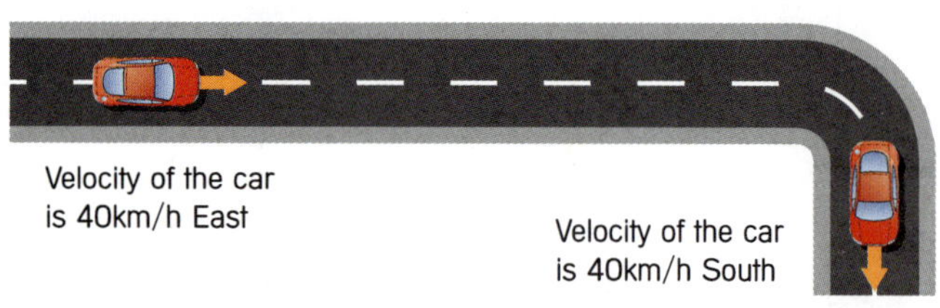

Acceleration

The **acceleration** of an object is the **rate** at which its **velocity changes**. It is a measure of how quickly an object **speeds up** or **slows down**.

To work out the acceleration of any moving object, you need to know...

- the **change in velocity**
- the **time taken** for this change in velocity.

The cyclist below increases his velocity by 2 metres per second every second. So, his acceleration is $2m/s^2$.

- **His velocity increases** by the **same amount** every second.
- The **actual distance** travelled each **second increases**.

You can calculate acceleration by using this formula:

$$\text{Acceleration } (m/s^2) = \frac{\text{Change in velocity (m/s)}}{\text{Time taken for change (s)}}$$

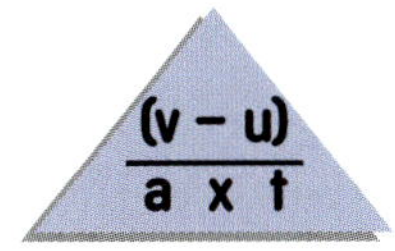

where v is the final velocity and u is the starting velocity

Deceleration is a negative acceleration. It describes an object that is **slowing down**. It is calculated using the same formula.

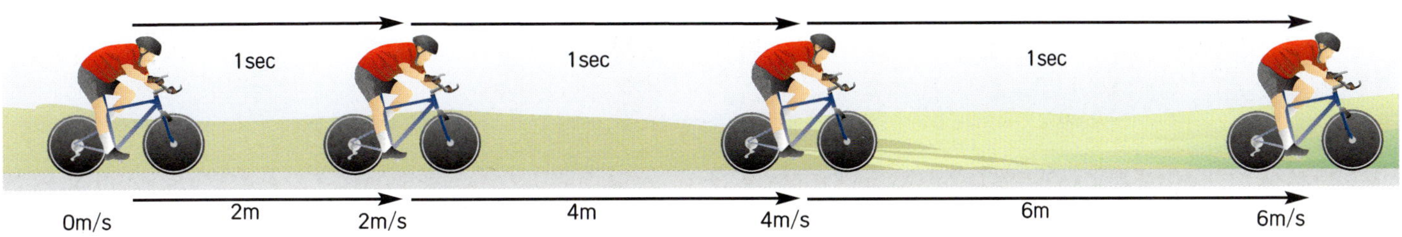

Velocity–Time Graphs

The **slope** of a **velocity–time graph** represents the **acceleration of the object**. The steeper the slope, the greater the acceleration.

The area **underneath** the line in a velocity–time graph represents the **total distance travelled**.

1. This graph shows an object moving at a constant speed of 10m/s. The object **isn't** accelerating.
2. This graph shows an object moving at a constant acceleration of $2m/s^2$.
3. This graph shows an object moving at a constant acceleration of $-3m/s^2$.

1

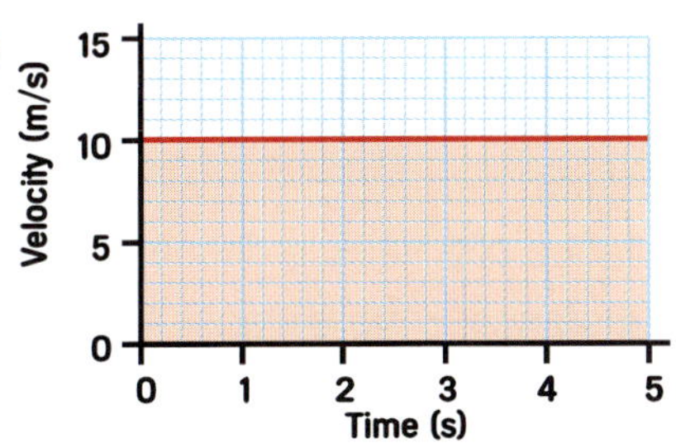

2

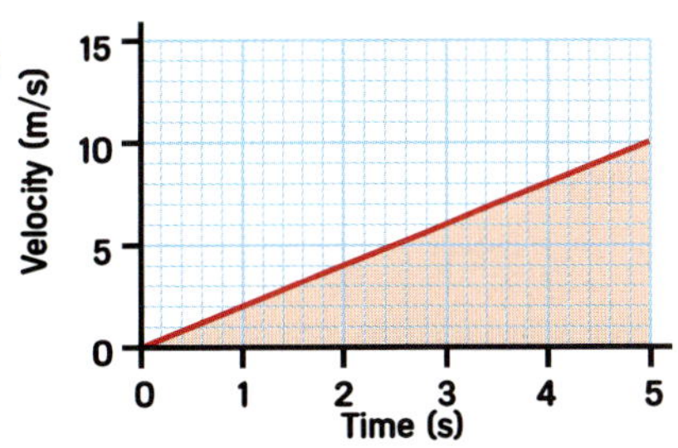

$\frac{10-0}{5} = 2m/s^2$

3

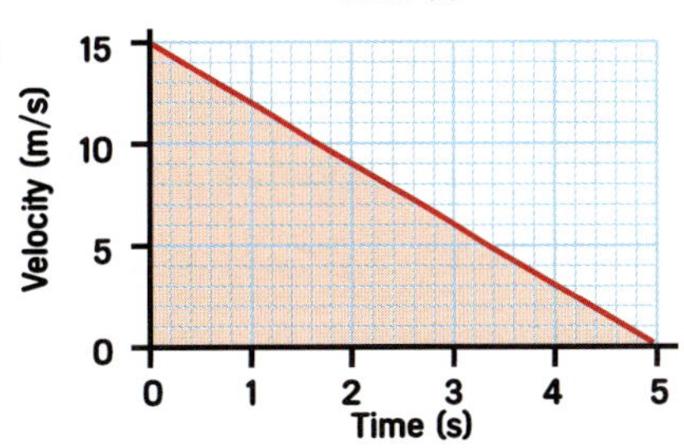

$\frac{0-15}{5} = -3m/s^2$

Key Words

Acceleration • Deceleration • Distance • Distance–time graph • Speed • Velocity • Velocity–time graph

Forces

Forces

Forces are pushes or pulls. They are measured in **newtons** (N) and may...

- vary in size
- act in different directions.

When a stationary object rests on a surface it exerts a **downward force** (weight). The surface it rests on exerts an **upward force** (reaction).

These two forces are **equal and opposite** and the object remains stationary.

A number of forces acting on an object can be replaced by a **single force**. This force has the **same effect** on the object as the **original forces** all **acting together**. This is called the **resultant force**.

Friction

Friction is a force that occurs when...

- an object moves through a medium, e.g. air or water
- surfaces slide past each other.

Friction works **against the object**, in the opposite direction to which it is moving.

When a motor vehicle travels at a steady speed, the **frictional forces balance the driving force**.

Stopping Distance

The stopping distance of a vehicle depends on...

- the **thinking distance** – the distance travelled by the vehicle during the driver's reaction time
- the **braking distance** – the distance travelled by the vehicle under the braking force.

The overall stopping distance is increased if:

- The vehicle is travelling at **greater speeds**.
- There are **adverse weather conditions**, e.g. wet or icy roads, poor visibility.
- The **driver is tired**, or under the influence of **drugs or alcohol** and can't react as quickly as normal.
- The **vehicle** is in a **poor condition**, e.g. it has under-inflated tyres.

The **greater the speed** of the vehicle, the **greater the braking force** needed to stop it in a certain time.

Thinking distance + **Braking distance** = **Stopping distance**

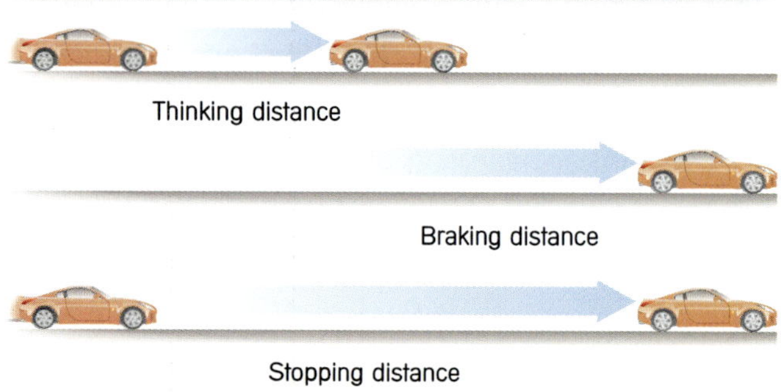

Key Words

Force • Friction • Newton • Resultant force

How Forces Affect Movement

The **movement** of an object depends on the **forces** acting on it.

If the forces are **equal and opposite** then they are **balanced**, i.e. the resultant force is **zero**.

If the forces are **not equal and opposite** then they are **unbalanced**, i.e. the resultant force is **not zero**.

If the resultant force acting on a **stationary** object is...

1. **zero**, the object will remain stationary
2. **not zero**, the object will start to move in the direction of the resultant force.

If the resultant force acting on a **moving object** is...

3. **zero**, the object will continue at the same speed in the same direction
4. **not zero**, the object will speed up or slow down in the direction of the resultant force.

1

2

3

4

Force, Mass & Acceleration

Force, Mass and Acceleration

If an unbalanced force acts on an object, the **acceleration** of the object will depend on...

- the **size** of the unbalanced force – the bigger the force, the greater the acceleration
- the **mass** of the object – the bigger the mass, the smaller the acceleration.

Example

One boy pushes a trolley. He exerts an unbalanced force which causes the trolley to move and accelerate.

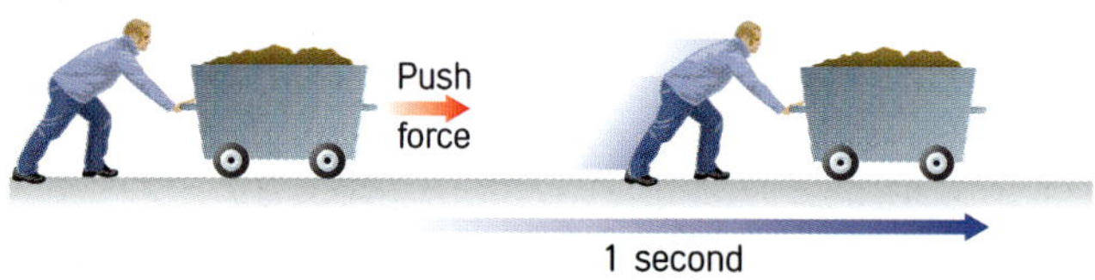

Two boys now push the same trolley. The trolley moves with a greater acceleration.

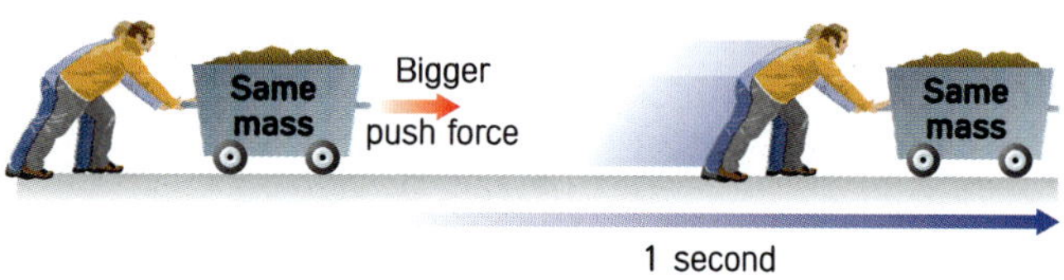

One boy pushes a trolley of bigger mass. It moves with a smaller acceleration than the first trolley.

The relationship between force, mass and acceleration is shown in this formula...

Resultant force (N) = Mass (kg) x Acceleration (m/s^2)

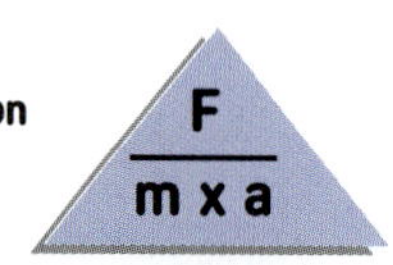

So, a **newton** (N) is the force needed to give a mass of one kilogram an acceleration of one metre per second squared (1 m/s^2).

Example

A trolley of mass 400kg is pushed along a floor with a constant speed by one boy who exerts a push force of 150N.

Another boy joins him to increase the push force, and the trolley accelerates at 0.5 m/s^2.

Calculate...

a) the force needed to achieve this acceleration

b) the total push force exerted on the trolley.

Initially the trolley is moving at a constant speed, so the forces acting on it must be balanced.

So, the 150N push force must be opposed by an equal force, i.e. friction or air resistance.

When the trolley starts accelerating, the push force must be greater than friction, etc. These forces don't cancel each other out and an unbalanced force now acts.

a) Force = Mass x Acceleration
= 400kg x 0.5 m/s^2
= 200N

b) Total push = Force needed to equal friction + Force needed to provide acceleration
= 150N + 200N
= 350N

Key Words

Acceleration • Mass • Newton • Resistance • Resultant force • Terminal velocity • Weight

Terminal Velocity

Falling objects experience two forces...
- the **downward force of weight**, W (↓)
- the **upward force of air resistance**, R, or drag (↑).

Weight always stays the same, but the force of air resistance changes.

Gravity is a force of attraction that acts between objects that have mass, e.g. a falling object and the Earth. The weight of an object is the force exerted on it by gravity. It is measured in **newtons** (N).

If a skydiver, Nick, jumps out of an aeroplane, the speed of his descent can be considered in two separate parts:
- before the parachute opens
- after the parachute opens.

Before the Parachute Opens

1. Immediately after Nick jumps, he accelerates due to the force of **gravity**.
2. As he falls, he experiences the **frictional force of air resistance** (R) in the opposite direction. At this point **weight** (W) is greater than R, so he continues to accelerate.
3. As his speed increases, so does R.
4. R increases until it is equal to W. The **resultant force** acting on Nick is now zero and his falling speed becomes **constant**. This speed is called the **terminal velocity**.

After the Parachute Opens

5. When the parachute opens, the force of R is now greatly increased and is bigger than W.
6. The increase in R decreases Nick's speed. As his speed decreases, so does R.
7. R decreases until it is equal to W. The forces acting are once again balanced and, for the second time, he falls at a steady speed, although slower than before. This is a **new terminal velocity**.

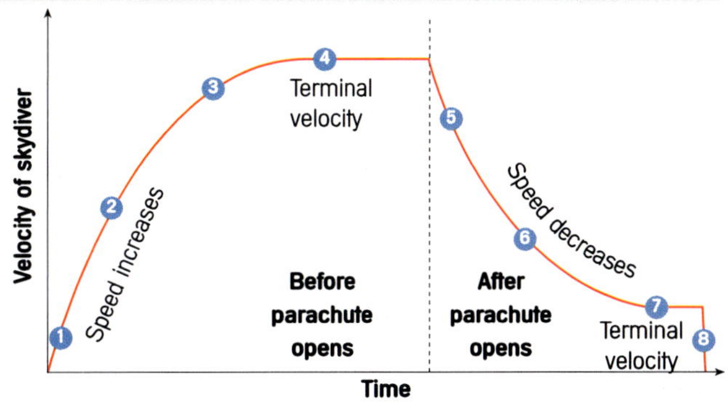

Work & Kinetic Energy

Work

When a force moves an object, **work** is **done** on the object resulting in the **transfer** of **energy**.

Energy is measured in joules (J). So...

Work done (J) = Energy transferred (J)

The relationship between work done, force and distance is shown by this formula:

Work done (J) = Force applied (N) X Distance moved in direction of force (m)

$$\frac{W}{F \times d}$$

Example
A man pushes a car with a steady force of 250N. The car moves a distance of 20m. How much work does the man do?

Work done = Force applied x Distance moved
= 250N x 20m
= **5000J (or 5kJ)**

Work done against frictional forces is mainly transformed into **heat energy**. When work is done on an elastic object to change its shape, the energy is stored in the object as **elastic potential energy**.

Kinetic Energy

Kinetic energy is the energy an object has because of its **movement**. It depends on two things:

- the **mass** of the object (kg)
- the **speed** of the object (m/s).

A moving car has kinetic energy as it has **both mass and speed**. As it moves with a **greater speed**, its mass is unchanged but it has **more kinetic energy**.

However, a moving truck has a **greater mass** than the car. So, even if it is going slower than the car, it may have **more kinetic energy**.

HT You can calculate kinetic energy by using this formula:

Kinetic energy (J) = $\frac{1}{2}$ X Mass (kg) X Speed^2 (m/s)^2

$$\frac{K.E.}{\frac{1}{2} \times m \times v^2}$$

Example
A car of mass 1000kg is moving at a speed of 10m/s. How much kinetic energy does it have?

Kinetic energy = $\frac{1}{2}$x Mass x Speed^2
= $\frac{1}{2}$x 1000kg x (10m/s)^2
= **50 000J (or 50kJ)**

Momentum

Momentum is a measure of the state of **motion** of an object. It depends on two things:

- the **mass** of the object (kg)
- the **velocity** of the object (m/s).

A moving car has momentum as it has **both mass and velocity**. If the car moves with a **greater velocity**, it will have **more momentum** providing its mass hasn't changed.

However, a moving truck with a greater mass may have more momentum than the car even if its velocity is less.

You can calculate momentum by using this formula:

Momentum (kg m/s) = Mass (kg) X Velocity (m/s)

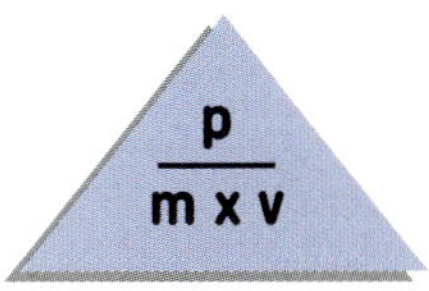

where p is momentum

Example 1

Calculate the momentum of a car of mass 1200kg that is travelling at a velocity of 30m/s.

Momentum = Mass x Velocity
= 1200kg x 30m/s
= **36 000kg m/s**

Example 2

A truck has a mass of 4000kg. Calculate its velocity if it has the same momentum as the car in Example 1.

Rearrange the formula...

$$\text{Velocity} = \frac{\text{Momentum}}{\text{Mass}} = \frac{36\,000\text{kg m/s}}{4000\text{kg}}$$

= **9m/s**

*N.B. Since the truck has a **greater mass** than the car, it can move at a **slower speed** and still have the **same momentum**.*

Magnitude and Direction

Momentum has...

- **magnitude** (size)
- **direction**.

The direction of movement is especially important when calculating momentum. For example...

- car A (moving from left to right) has a positive velocity and, consequently, a positive momentum
- car B (moving from right to left) has a negative velocity and negative momentum because it is moving in the opposite direction to car A.

Examples

Car A has a mass of 1000kg and a velocity of 20m/s. Calculate its momentum.

Momentum = 1000kg x 20m/s
= **20 000kg m/s**

Car B has a mass of 1000kg and a velocity of -20m/s. Calculate its momentum.

Momentum = 1000kg x -20m/s
= **-20 000kg m/s**

Key Words

Energy • Kinetic energy • Mass • Momentum • Speed • Transfer • Velocity • Work

Momentum

Force and Change in Momentum

When a **force** acts on a **moving object**, or a stationary object that is capable of moving, the object will experience a **change** in **momentum**.

An external force can...

- give a stationary object **momentum**
- **increase** the momentum of a moving object
- **decrease**, or stop, the momentum of a moving object.

The extent of the change in momentum depends on...

- the **size** of the force
- the **length** of time the force is acting on the object.

HT Force, change in momentum and the time taken for the change are related by this formula:

$$\text{Force (N)} = \frac{\text{Change in momentum (kg m/s)}}{\text{Time taken for change (s)}}$$

where $\Delta(mv)$ is change in momentum

$$\frac{\Delta(mv)}{F \times t}$$

Example

A girl kicks a stationary ball with a force of 30N. The force acts on the ball for 0.15 seconds. The mass of the ball is 0.5kg.

a) Calculate the change in momentum of the ball

Change in momentum = Force x Time
= 30N x 0.15s
= **4.5kg m/s**

b) Calculate the increase in velocity of the ball.

$$\text{Velocity} = \frac{\text{Momentum}}{\text{Mass}} = \frac{4.5\text{kg m/s}}{0.5\text{kg}} = \mathbf{9m/s}$$

The girl can **increase** the **change in momentum** of the ball, and as a result its **velocity**, without increasing the force applied. She can do this by 'following through' with her kick. This will **increase the time** for which the **force is applied**.

Some sports where 'following through' increases the velocity of the ball are...

- football
- cricket
- golf
- tennis
- squash.

Collisions & Explosions

Collisions and Explosions

In any collision or explosion, the **momentum** in a particular direction **after the event** is the same as the momentum in that direction **before the event**.

Momentum is conserved, provided that no external forces act.

Example 1

Two cars are travelling in the same direction along a road. Car A collides with the back of car B and they stick together. Calculate their velocity after the collision.

Before

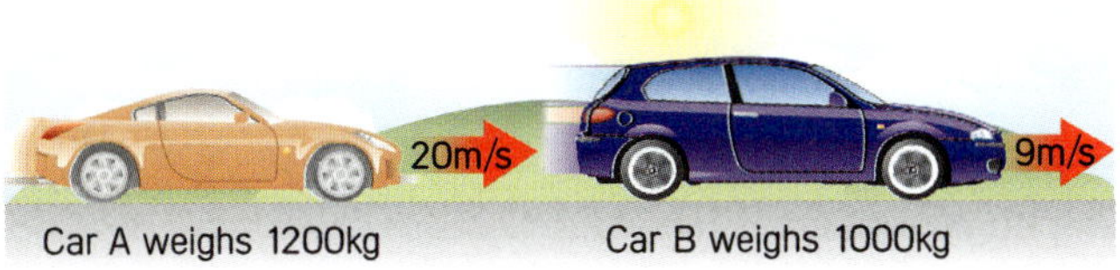

After

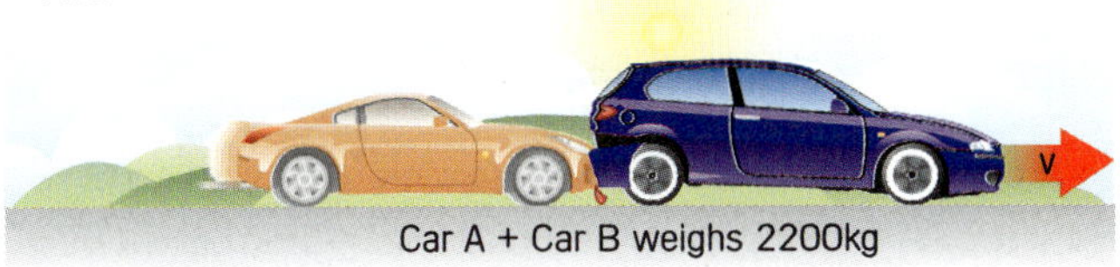

Momentum before collision:

= Momentum of A + Momentum of B
= (Mass x velocity of A) + (Mass x velocity of B)
= (1200kg x 20m/s) + (1000kg x 9m/s)
= 24 000kg m/s + 9000kg m/s
= 33 000kg m/s

Momentum after collision:

= Momentum of A and B
= (Mass of A + Mass of B) x (Velocity of A + B)
= (1200+1000) x v
= 2200v

Since momentum is conserved:

Total momentum before = Total momentum after

33 000 = 2200v

$$\text{So, } v = \frac{33\,000}{2200}$$

= **15m/s**

Example 2

A gun fires a bullet of mass 0.01 kg. The velocity of the bullet is 350m/s. Calculate the recoil velocity of the gun.

Before **After**

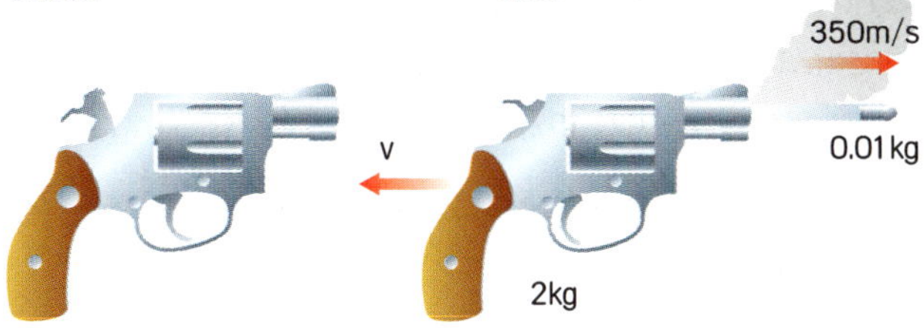

Firing a gun is an example of an explosion where two objects move **away** from each other.

Since the gun and the bullet are moving in opposite directions, we will assume that the **bullet** has **positive** velocity and momentum which means that the **gun** has **negative** velocity and momentum.

Momentum before explosion = 0
(Neither the gun nor the bullet are moving.)

Momentum after explosion:

= Momentum of bullet + Momentum of gun
= (Mass x velocity of bullet) + (Mass x velocity of gun)
= (0.01 kg x 350m/s) + (2kg x -v)
= 3.5 − 2v

Remember the gun has negative velocity

Since momentum is conserved:

Momentum after explosion = Momentum before explosion
Momentum of bullet + Momentum of gun = 0
(Mass x velocity of bullet) + (Mass x velocity of gun) = 0
(0.01 kg x 350m/s) + (2kg x v) = 0
3.5 + 2v = 0
2v = -3.5

$$v = \frac{3.5}{2}$$

v = **-1.75m/s**

Key Words

Force • Momentum • Velocity

Static Electricity

Static Electricity

Some insulating materials can become **electrically charged** when they are rubbed against each other. Unless it is **discharged**, the electrical charge (static) stays on the material.

Static electricity builds up when **electrons** (negative charge) are 'rubbed off' one material onto another. The material...

- **receiving** electrons becomes **negatively** charged
- **giving up** electrons becomes **positively** charged.

Examples

A perspex rod rubbed with cloth loses electrons to become positively charged. The cloth gains electrons to become negatively charged.

An ebonite rod rubbed with fur gains electrons to become negatively charged. The fur loses electrons to become positively charged.

Repulsion and Attraction

When two charged materials are brought together, they **exert a force** on each other. They are either **attracted** or **repelled**:

- Materials with the **same** charge **repel** each other.
- Materials with **different** charges **attract** each other.

Examples

If a charged perspex rod is moved near to a suspended perspex rod, the suspended perspex rod will be repelled.

If a charged ebonite rod is moved near to a suspended charged perspex rod, the suspended perspex rod will be attracted.

The Uses of Static

Electrostatic charges can be very useful in industry and at home. They can be used in a variety of different ways.

Examples

Reducing air pollution in **electrostatic smoke precipitators**, and reproducing images in **photocopiers**.

Electrostatic Smoke Precipitator

Smoke precipitators are designed to remove solid smoke particles from waste gases before the gases are released into the environment:

1. Solid smoke particles become positively charged as they pass by a charged metal grid.
2. These 'like' charges repel each other causing the particles to move away from the grid.
3. The particles are then attracted to the negatively charged collecting plates. The particles stick to form a layer of 'soot' which is regularly removed.

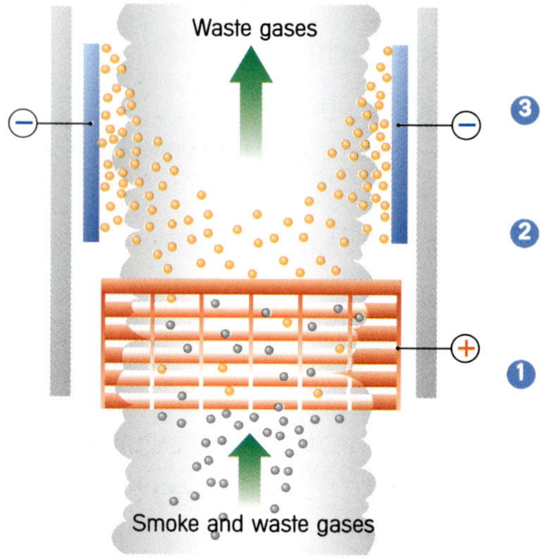

The Photocopier

1. An image of the page to be copied is projected onto an electrically charged plate (usually positively charged).
2. Light causes charge to leak away leaving an electrostatic impression of the page.
3. The charged impression on the plate attracts tiny specks of black powder. The powder is then transferred from the plate to paper. Heat is used to fix the final image on the paper.

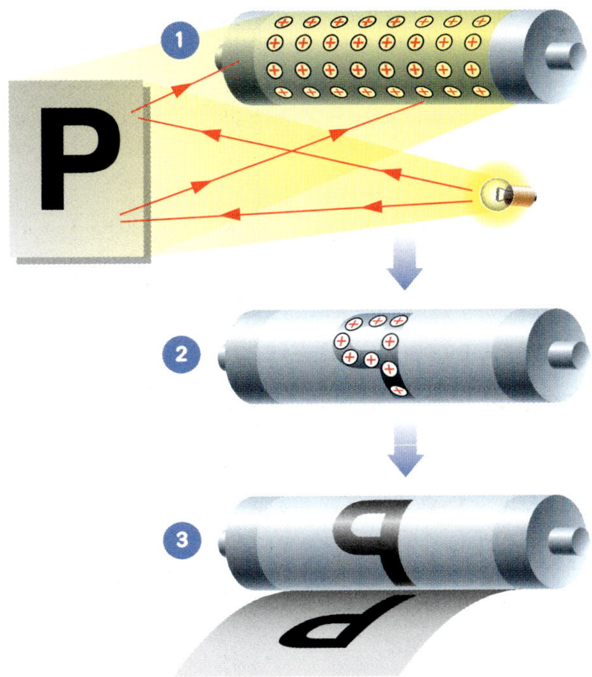

Key Words

Attraction • Charged • Current • Electron • Electrostatic• Potential difference • Repulsion • Static electricity

Discharge of Static Electricity

A **charged conductor** (positive or negative) can be **discharged**. Any charge on it is **removed** by connecting it to earth with a conductor.

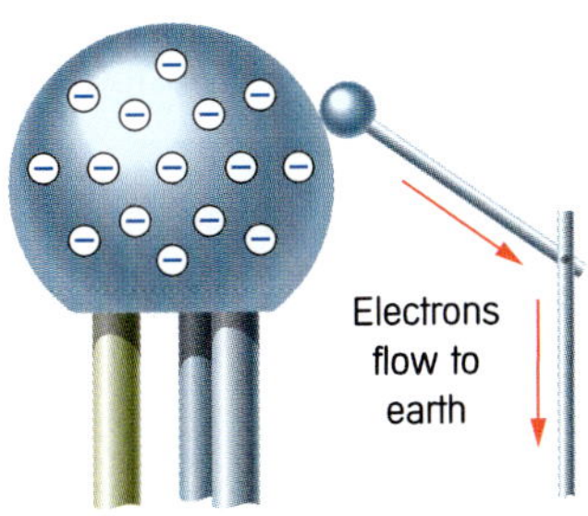

If a conductor touches a negatively charged dome, electrons flow from the dome to earth, via the conductor, until the dome is completely discharged.

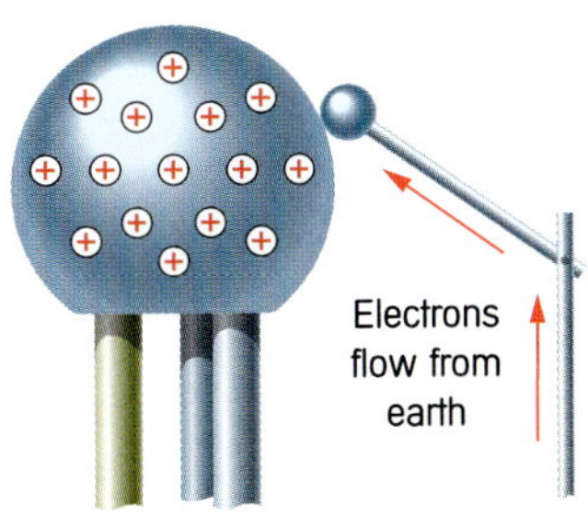

If a conductor touches a positively charged dome, electrons flow from earth to cancel out the positive charge on the dome, until the dome is completely discharged.

This flow of electrons through a solid conductor is an **electric current**.

Metals **conduct electricity** well because electrons from their **atoms** can **move freely** throughout the metal structure.

HT The greater the charge on an isolated object, the greater the potential difference between the object and earth.

If the potential difference between the object and a nearby earthed conductor becomes high enough, the air molecules can **ionise**, and there is a spark as **discharge** occurs.

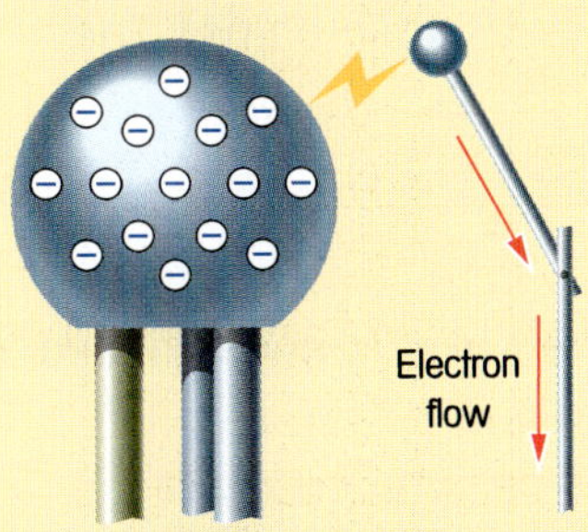

If an earthed conductor is near a dome with a high negative charge, electrons flow from the dome through the air to get to earth via the conductor.

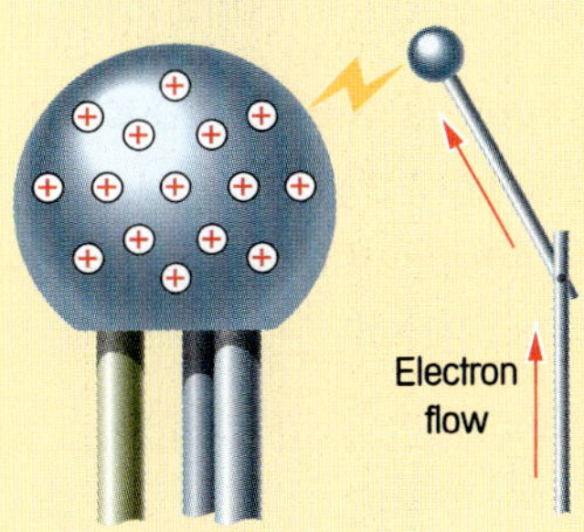

If an earthed conductor is near a dome with a high positive charge, electrons flow from the dome through the air to cancel out the positive charge on the dome.

Electric Circuits

Circuits

An electric current will flow through an electrical component (or device) if there is a potential difference (voltage) across the ends of the component.

In a circuit...

- the potential difference (p.d.) is measured in **volts (V)** using a **voltmeter** connected in **parallel**
- the **current** is measured in amperes (A), using an ammeter connected in series.

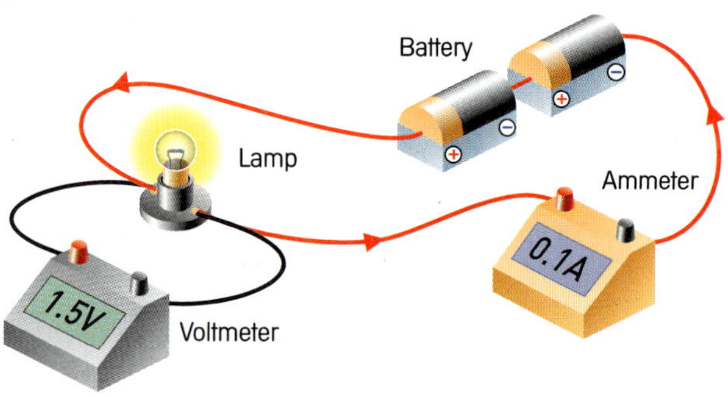

The amount of current that flows through the component depends on...

- the potential difference across the component
- the resistance of the component.

The **greater the potential difference** across a component, the **greater the current** that flows through the component.

Components resist the flow of current through them. They have resistance (measured in ohms). The greater the resistance of a component(s)...

- the smaller the current that flows for a particular potential difference
- **or** the greater the potential difference needed to maintain a particular current.

N.B. In the following circuits, each cell and lamp are identical.

Circuit 1

The cell provides p.d. across the lamp. A current flows and the lamp lights up.

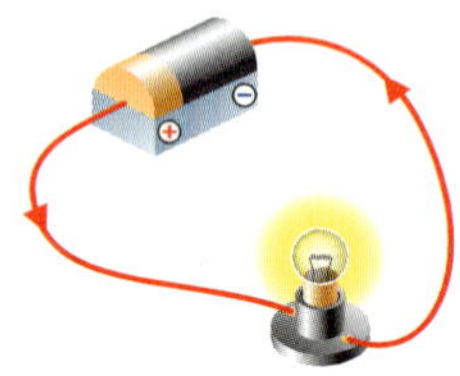

Circuit 2

Two cells together provide a bigger p.d. across the lamp. A bigger current flows and the lamp lights up more brightly (compared to circuit 1).

Circuit 3

Two lamps together have a greater resistance. A smaller current now flows and the lamps light up less brightly (compared to circuit 1).

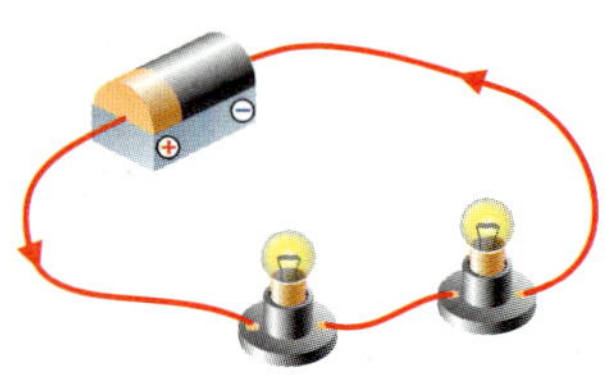

Circuit 4

Two cells together provide a greater p.d. The same current as in circuit 1 now flows. The lamps light up as brightly as in circuit 1.

Key Words

Current • Diode • Potential difference • Resistance • Resistor • Thermistor

Resistance

Resistance is a measure of **how hard** it is to **get a current** through a **component** at a particular potential difference.

Current–potential difference graphs show how the current through the component varies with the potential difference across it.

Potential difference, current and resistance are related by this formula:

Potential difference (volt, V) = **Current (ampere, A)** x **Resistance (ohm,)**

where I is current

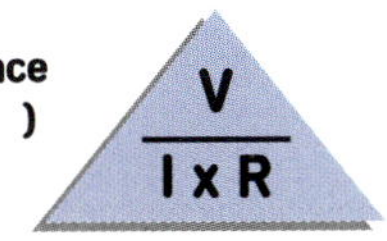

Resistors

The resistance of a **light dependent resistor (LDR)** depends on the amount of light falling on it. Its **resistance decreases** as the amount of **light** falling on it **increases**. This allows more current to flow.

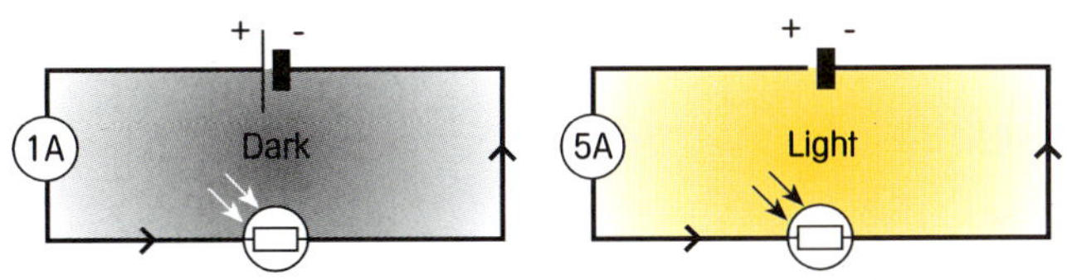

The resistance of a **thermistor** depends on its **temperature**. Its **resistance decreases** as the **temperature** of the thermistor **increases**. This allows more current to flow.

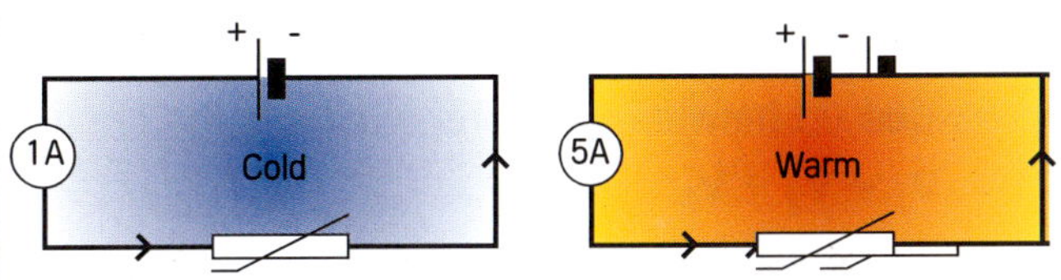

As long as the temperature of the **resistor** stays constant, the current through the resistor is directly proportional to the voltage across the resistor, i.e. if one doubles, the other also doubles. This is regardless of which direction the current is flowing.

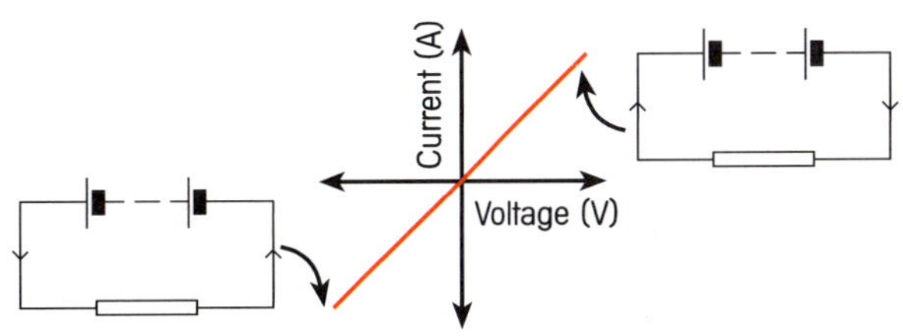

As the temperature of the **filament lamp** increases, and the bulb gets brighter, then the resistance of the lamp increases. This is regardless of which direction the current is flowing.

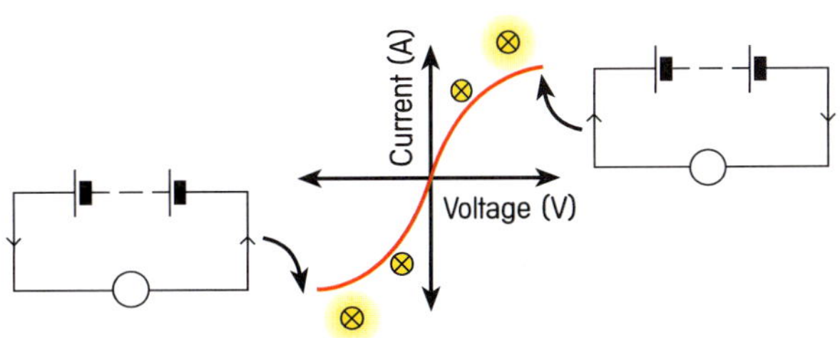

A **diode** allows a current to flow through it in **one direction only**. It has a very high resistance in the reverse direction so no current flows.

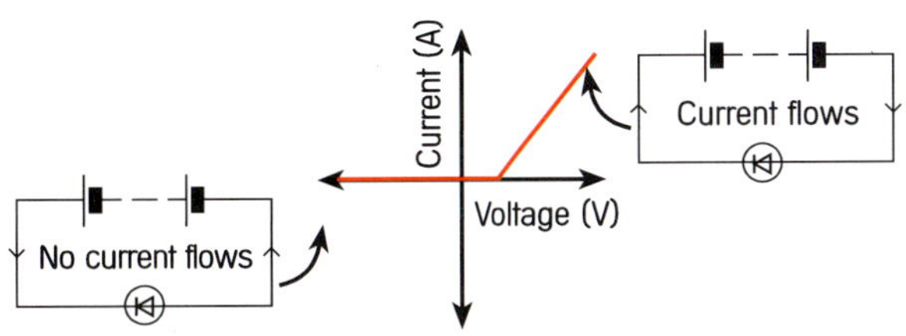

Electric Circuits

Series and Parallel Circuits

Connecting Components in Series

In a **series circuit**, all components are connected one after the other in one loop, going from one terminal of the battery to the other.

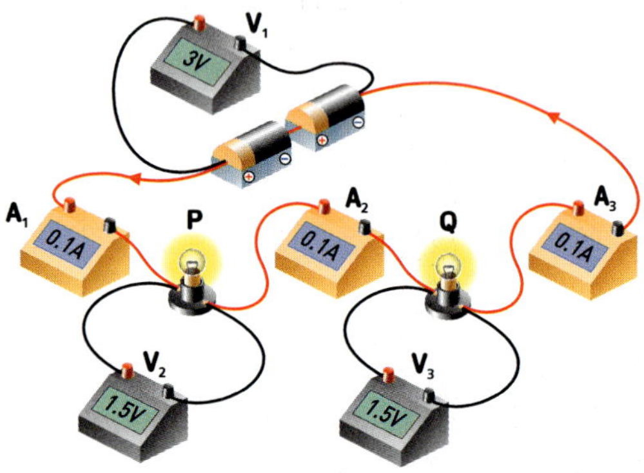

- The **same current** flows through each component, i.e. $\mathbf{A_1 = A_2 = A_3}$. In this circuit, each ammeter reading is 0.1A.
- The **potential difference** supplied by the battery is **divided** up between the components in the circuit, i.e. $\mathbf{V_1 = V_2 + V_3}$.
- In this circuit, both bulbs have the same resistance so the voltage is divided equally. If one bulb had twice the resistance of the other, then the voltage would be divided differently, e.g. 2V and 1V.
- The total resistance is the sum of the individual resistances of the components, i.e. $\Omega = \Omega_P + \Omega_Q$. If both P and Q each have a resistance of 15 ohms, the total resistance would be 15 ohms + 15 ohms = 30 ohms.

Connecting Components in Parallel

In a **parallel circuit**, all components are connected separately in their own loop going from one terminal of the battery to the other.

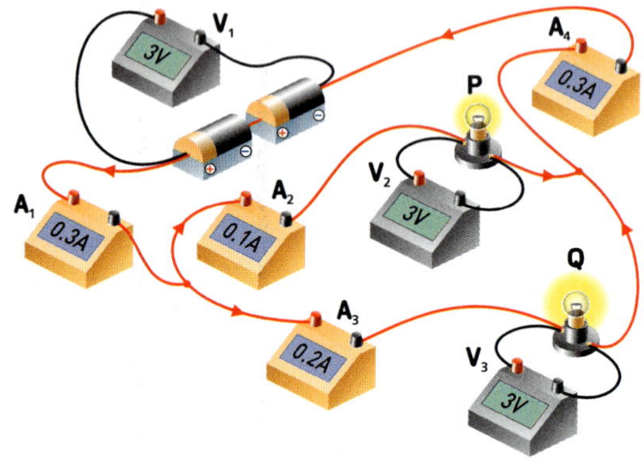

- The total current in the main circuit is equal to the sum of the currents through the separate components, i.e. $\mathbf{A_1 = A_2 + A_3 = A_4}$. In this circuit, 0.3A = 0.1A + 0.2A = 0.3A.
- The potential difference across each component is the same (and is equal to the p.d. of the battery), i.e. $\mathbf{V_1 = V_2 = V_3}$. In this circuit, each bulb has a p.d. of 3V across it.
- The amount of current which passes through a component depends on the resistance of the component. The greater the resistance, the smaller the current. Bulb P must have twice the resistance of bulb Q as only 0.1A passes through bulb P while 0.2A passes through bulb Q.

Connecting Cells in Series

The **total potential difference** provided by cells connected in series is the sum of the potential difference of each cell separately, providing that they have been connected in the same direction.

Each cell has a potential difference of 1.5V.

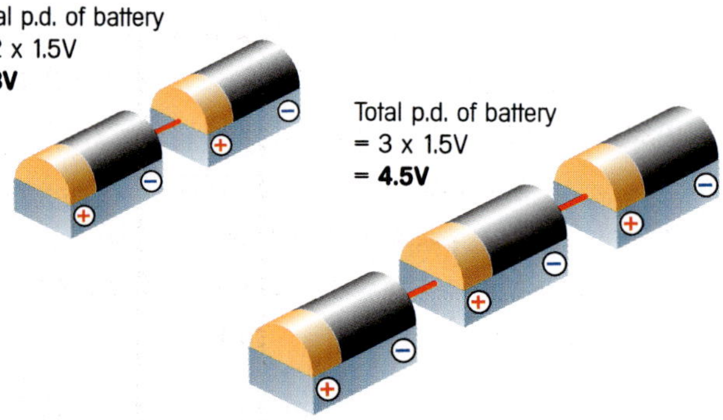

Currents

A **direct current** (d.c.) always flows in the **same direction**. Cells and batteries supply direct current.

An **alternating current** (a.c.) **changes the direction** of flow back and forth continuously.

The **frequency** is the number of complete cycles of reversal per second. The UK mains electricity is 50 cycles per second (Hertz).

The UK mains supply has a voltage of about **230 volts**. This voltage, if it isn't used safely, can kill.

The Three-Pin Plug

The 3-pin Plug

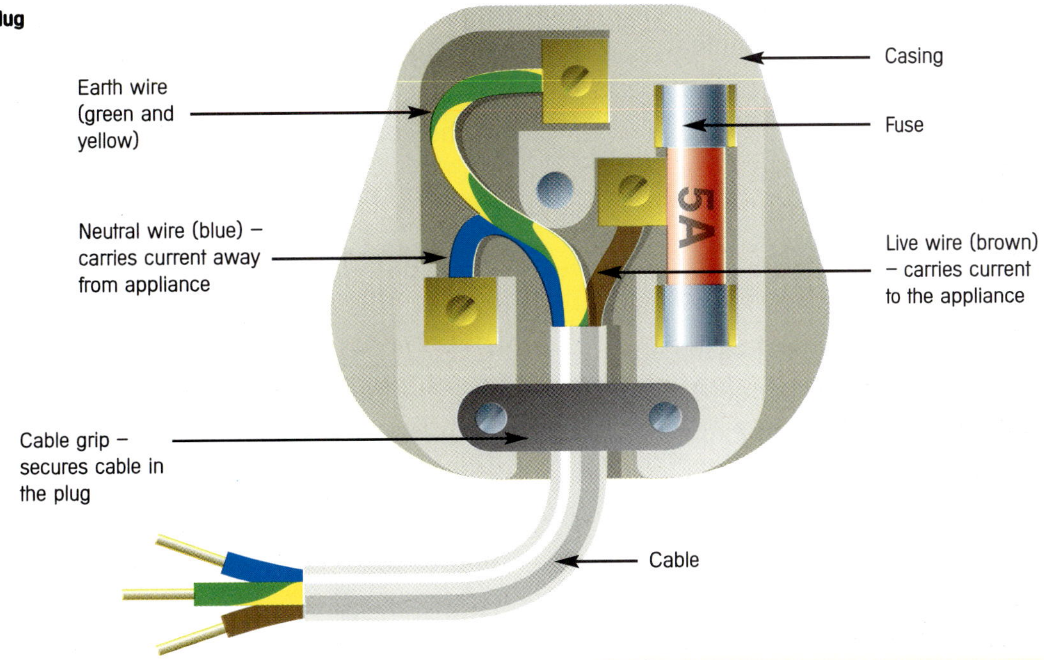

Most electrical appliances are connected to the mains electricity supply using a **cable** and a **three-pin plug**.

The plug is inserted into a socket on the ring main circuit.

The materials used for the plug and cable depend on their properties:

- The **inner cores** of the wires are made of **copper** because it's a **good conductor**.
- The **outer layers** are made of flexible **plastic** because it's a **good insulator**.
- The **pins** of a plug are made from **brass** because it's a **good conductor.**
- The **casing** is made from **plastic or rubber** because both are **good insulators**.

HT The live terminal of the mains supply alternates between a **positive** and **negative** voltage with respect to the neutral terminal.

The neutral terminal stays at a voltage close to zero with respect to Earth.

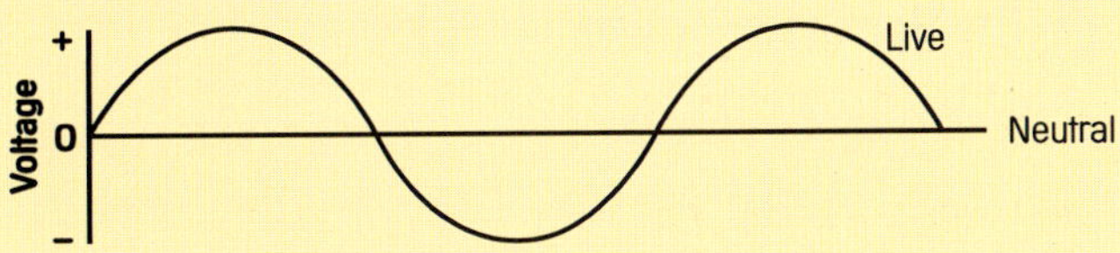

Key Words

Alternating current • Direct current • Frequency • Parallel circuit • Series circuit

Circuit Breakers & Fuses

Circuit Breakers and Fuses

If an electrical fault causes a **current that is too high**, the circuit will be **switched off** by a **circuit breaker** or **fuse**.

A **circuit breaker** is a safety device which **automatically breaks** an electric circuit if it becomes overloaded. Circuit breakers can be **easily reset** by pressing a button.

If the current becomes too high:

1. An electromagnet increases in strength.
2. The electromagnet separates a pair of contacts.
3. The circuit is broken ('trips').
4. The appliance or user is protected.

A **fuse** should always be part of a live circuit. It's a short, thin piece of wire with a **low melting point**.

The current rating of the fuse must be **just above** the normal working current of the appliance for the safety system to work properly.

If the current running through the appliance is greater than the current rating of the fuse:

1. The fuse wire gets hot and melts or breaks.
2. The circuit is broken.
3. The current is no longer able to flow.
4. The appliance or user is protected.

Earthing

Electrical appliances with outer **metal cases** are usually **earthed**. The outer case of an appliance is connected to the earth pin in the plug through the earth wire.

The **earth wire** and **fuse** work together to protect the appliance and the user.

If a fault in the appliance connects the live wire to the case...

1. The case will become live.
2. The current will then 'run to earth' through the earth wire as this offers least resistance.
3. This overload of current will cause the fuse to melt (or the circuit breaker to trip).
4. The appliance or user is protected.

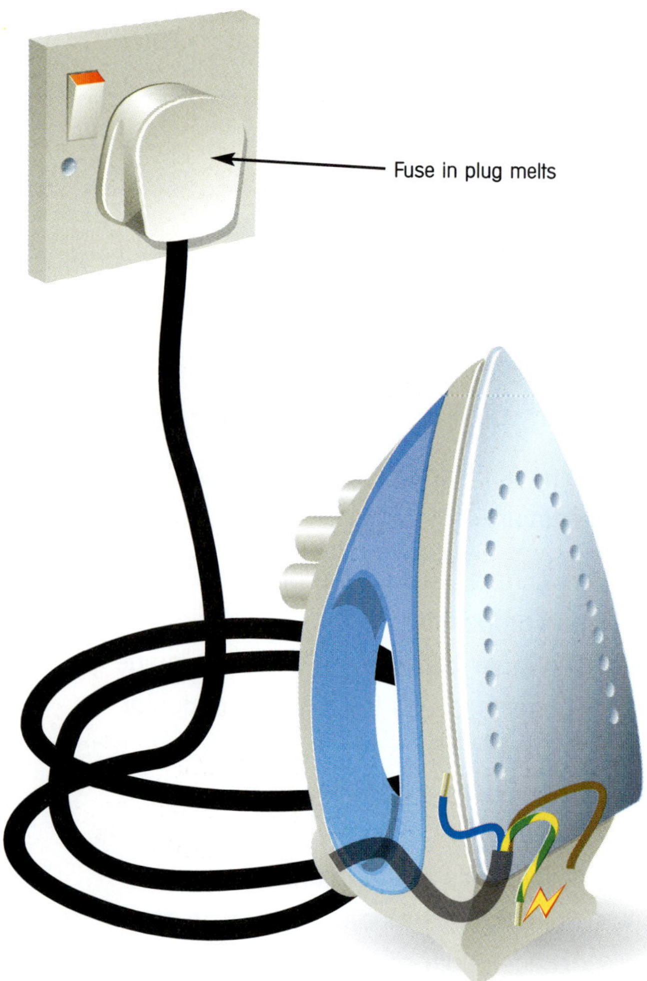

Key Words

Circuit breaker • Current • Earthed • Fuse • Potential difference • Resistor • Transform

Power

An electric **current** is the rate of **flow of charge**. A current transfers **electrical energy** from a battery or power supply to components in a **circuit**.

The rate of flow is measured in **amperes** (A).

The **components transform** some of this electrical energy into **other forms** of energy. For example, a **resistor** transforms **electrical** energy into **heat energy**.

The rate at which energy is transformed by a component or appliance is called the **power**.

You can calculate power by using this formula:

$$\text{Power (watt, W)} = \frac{\text{Energy transformed (joule, J)}}{\text{Time (second, s)}}$$

You can also calculate power using the formula:

$$\text{Power (watt, W)} = \text{Potential difference (volt, V)} \times \text{Current (ampere, A)}$$

where I is the current

$$\frac{P}{V \times I}$$

HT Charge

The **amount of electrical charge** which passes any point in a circuit is measured in **coulombs** (C).

You can calculate charge using this formula:

$$\text{Charge (coulomb, C)} = \text{Current (amp, A)} \times \text{Time (second, s)}$$

where Q is charge

$$\frac{Q}{I \times T}$$

Example:

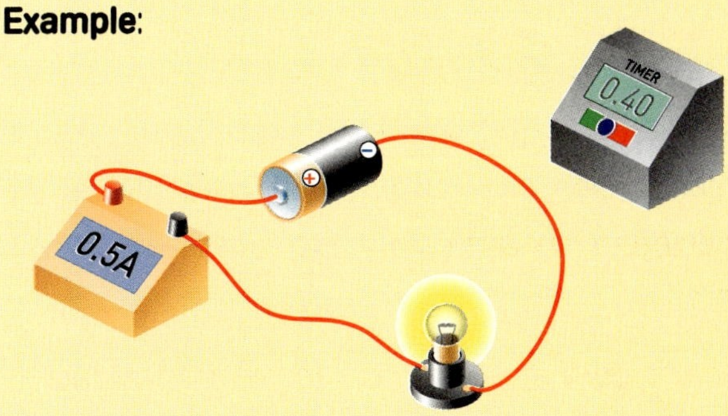

If the circuit above is switched on for 40 seconds and the current is 0.5 amps, what is the charge?

Charge = Current x Time
= 0.5A x 40s
= **20 coulombs**

Transforming Energy

As charge passes through a device, energy is **transformed**.

The **amount of energy** transformed for every coulomb of charge depends on the **size of the potential difference**. The greater the potential difference, the more energy transformed per coulomb.

Example:
If a circuit has a potential difference of 1.5V, and a charge of 23C, how much energy is transformed?

Energy transformed = p.d. x Charge
= 1.5V x 24C
= **36 joules**

Remember, the charge gained this energy from the battery. It was transformed to the bulb whilst the circuit was switched on.

Atoms & Radiation

Atoms

An atom is made up of three parts:

- **protons**
- **neutrons**
- **electrons**.

An atom has the **same number** of **protons** as **electrons**. So, an atom as a whole has no **electrical charge**.

All atoms of a particular element have the **same number of protons**.

Atoms of different elements have **different numbers of protons**.

The number of protons defines the element:

- The number of **protons** in an atom is called its **atomic number**.
- The number of **protons** and **neutrons** in an atom is called its **mass number**.

Some atoms of the same element can have **different numbers of neutrons**. These are called **isotopes**.

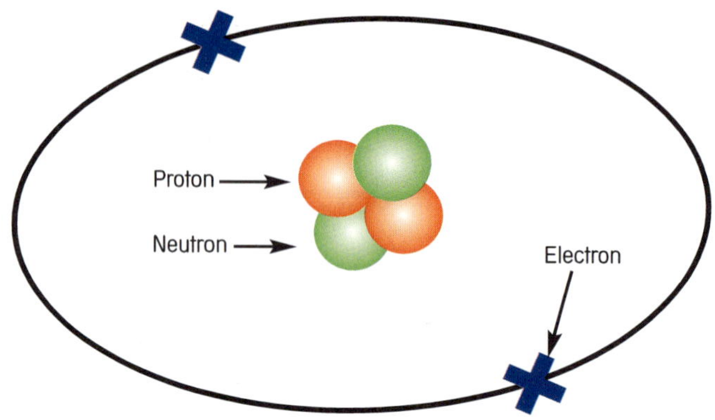

Atomic Particle	Relative Mass	Relative Change
Proton	1	+1
Neutron	1	0
Electron	0 (nearly)	-1

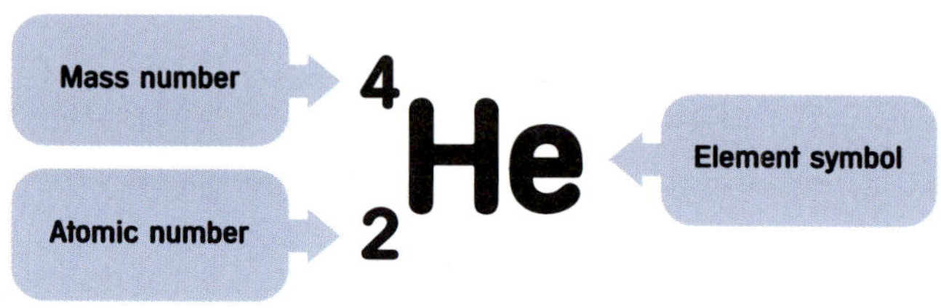

Radioactive Decay

Radioactive isotopes (radioisotopes or radionuclides) are atoms with **unstable nuclei**. They may disintegrate and emit **radiation**. This is **radioactive decay**.

This decay can result in the formation of a **different atom** with a **different number of protons**.

Two examples of this are...

- **alpha** (α) radiation
- **beta** (β) radiation.

There is also **gamma (γ) radiation**. However, unlike alpha and beta, gamma emissions have no effect on the structure of the nucleus.

Alpha Decay

In alpha decay, the original atom decays by ejecting an alpha particle from the nucleus.

An alpha particle is a **helium nucleus** – a particle made up of **two protons** and **two neutrons**.

A new atom is formed with α decay.

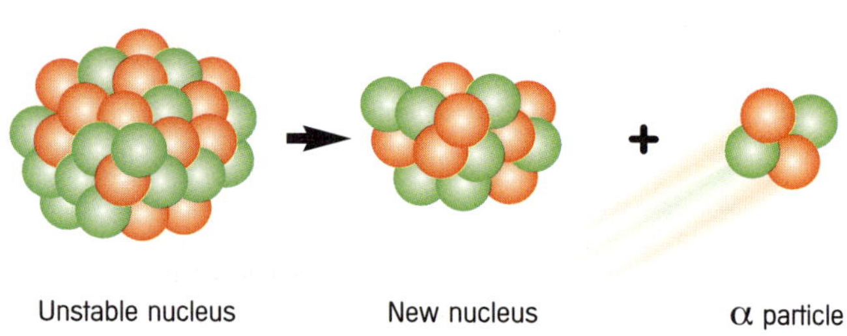

Beta Decay

In beta decay, the original atom decays by changing a **neutron** into a **proton** and an **electron**.

The newly formed high-energy electron ejected from the nucleus, is a β particle.

A new atom is formed with β decay.

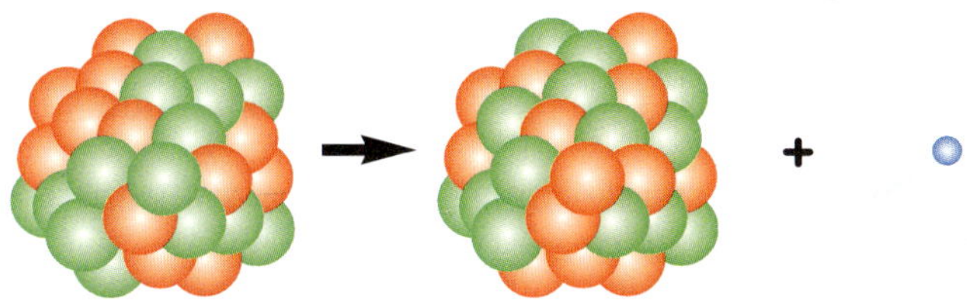

Ionisation

Radioactive particles can collide with **neutral** atoms or molecules. Electrons will be knocked out of their structure and they will become **charged**.

These charged particles are called ions. **Alpha** and **beta** radiation are known as **ionising radiation**.

This type of radiation can damage molecules in healthy cells. This can result in the death of the cell.

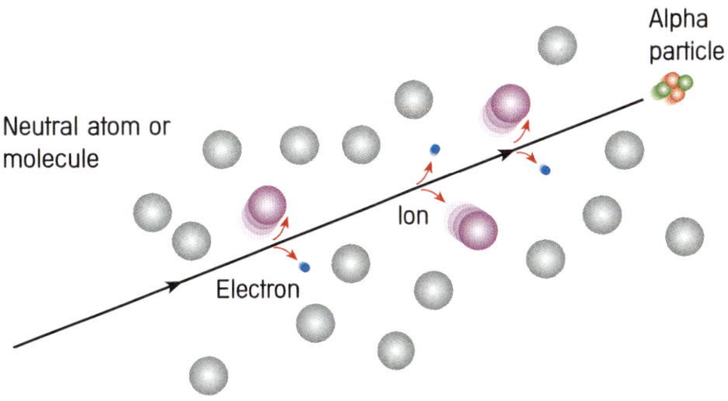

Background Radiation

Background radiation is not harmful to our health as it occurs in very small doses.

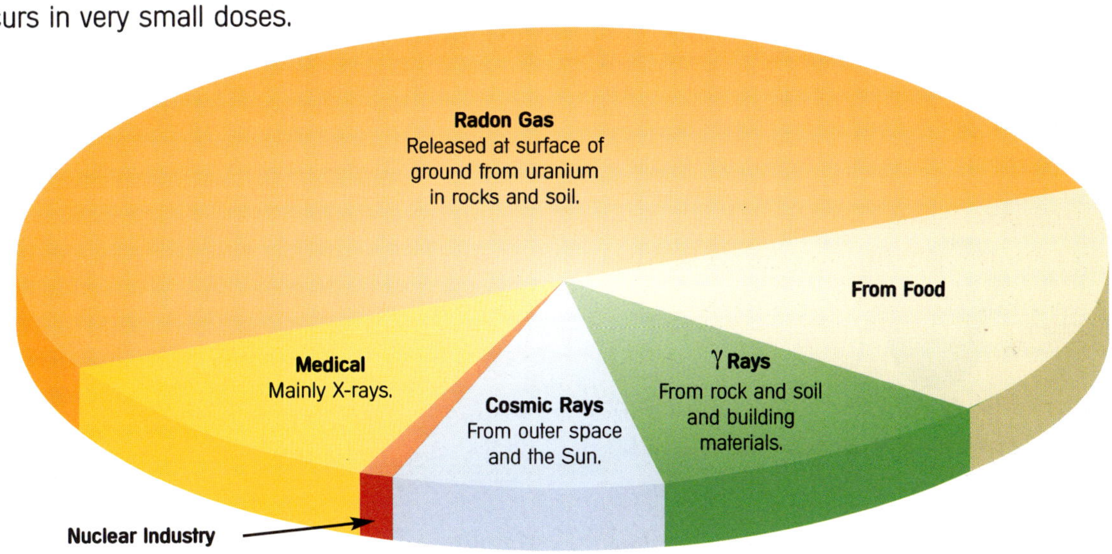

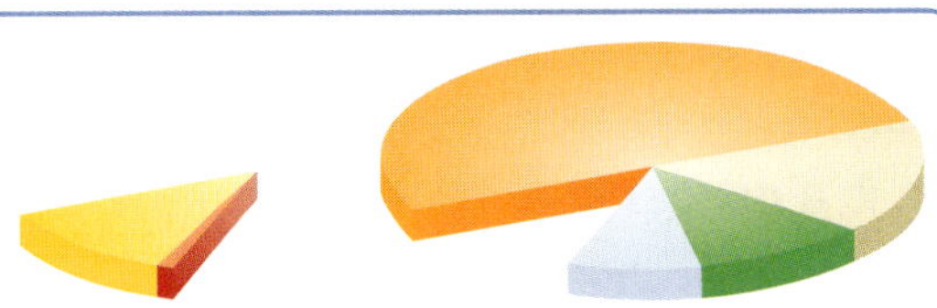

Key Words

Atomic number • Electron • Ion • Isotope • Mass number • Neutron • Proton • Radiation

Nuclear Fusion & Fission

Nuclear Fusion

Nuclear fusion is the **joining together** of two or more atomic nuclei to form a **larger atomic nucleus**.

A lot of energy is needed for the nuclei to fuse.

A nuclear fusion reaction generally releases more energy than it uses. This makes it **self-sustaining**, i.e. some of the energy produced is used to drive further fusion reactions.

An example of nuclear fusion is the fusion of two heavy forms of hydrogen (deuterium and tritium).

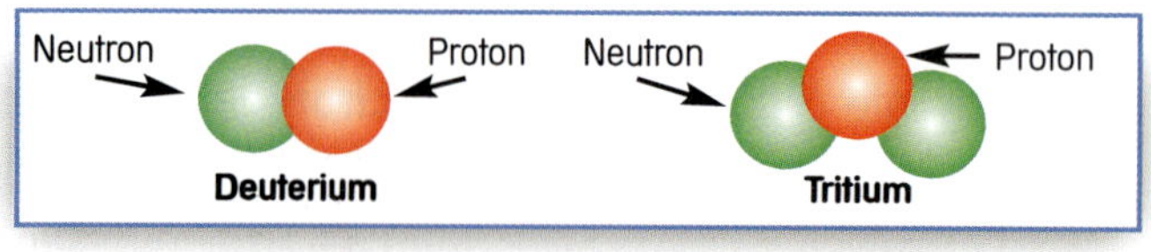

When they are forced together, the deuterium and tritium nuclei **fuse together** to form a **new helium atom** and an **unchanged neutron**.

Stars **release energy** by nuclear fusion. In the core of the Sun, **hydrogen** is **converted** to **helium** by fusion. This provides the energy to keep the Sun burning and allow life on Earth.

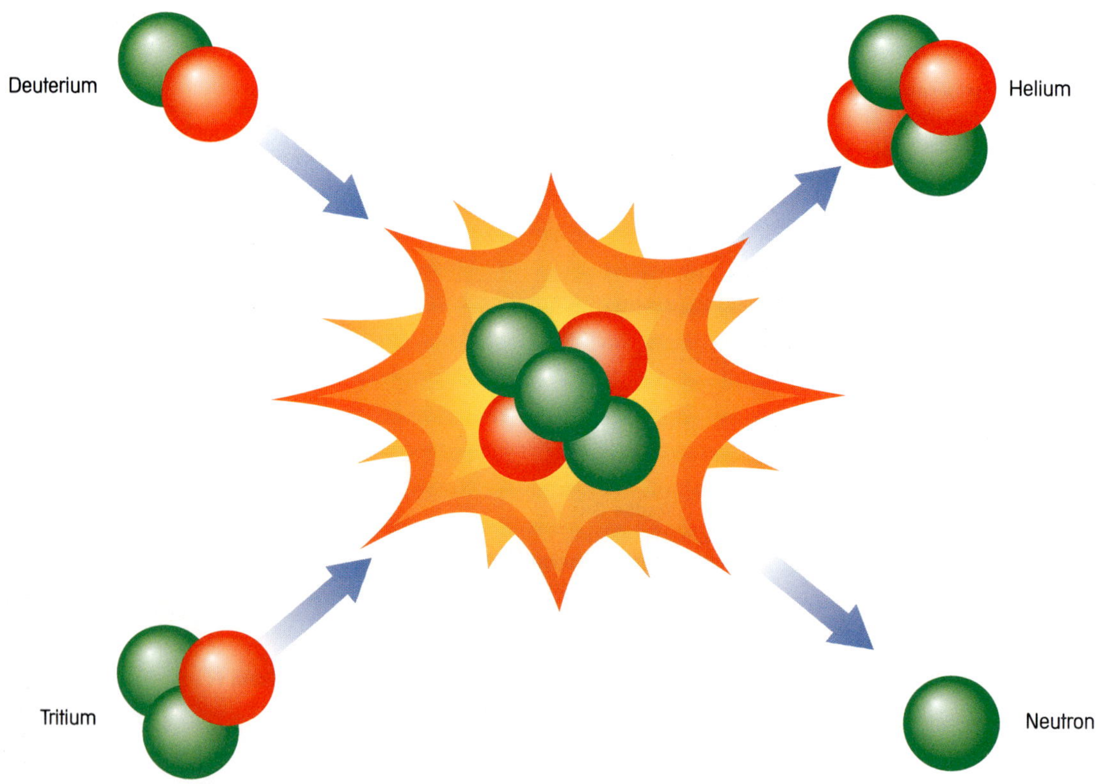

Nuclear Fission

Nuclear fission is the **splitting** of atomic nuclei. It is used in nuclear reactors to **produce energy** to make electricity.

Key Words

Nuclear fission • Nuclear fusion

The two substances most commonly used are **uranium-235** and **plutonium-239**.

The products of nuclear fission are **radioactive**. So, there is a **danger** of reactions potentially getting out of control (e.g. Chernobyl). But, one **benefit** is the large amount of energy that is released by an atom during nuclear fission.

Nuclear Fission On a Small Scale

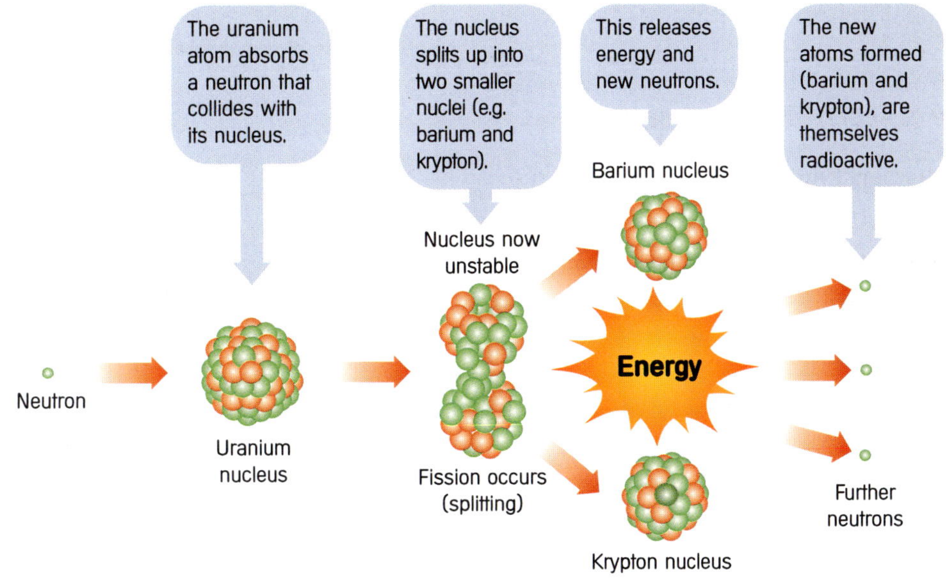

Nuclear Fission On a Large Scale

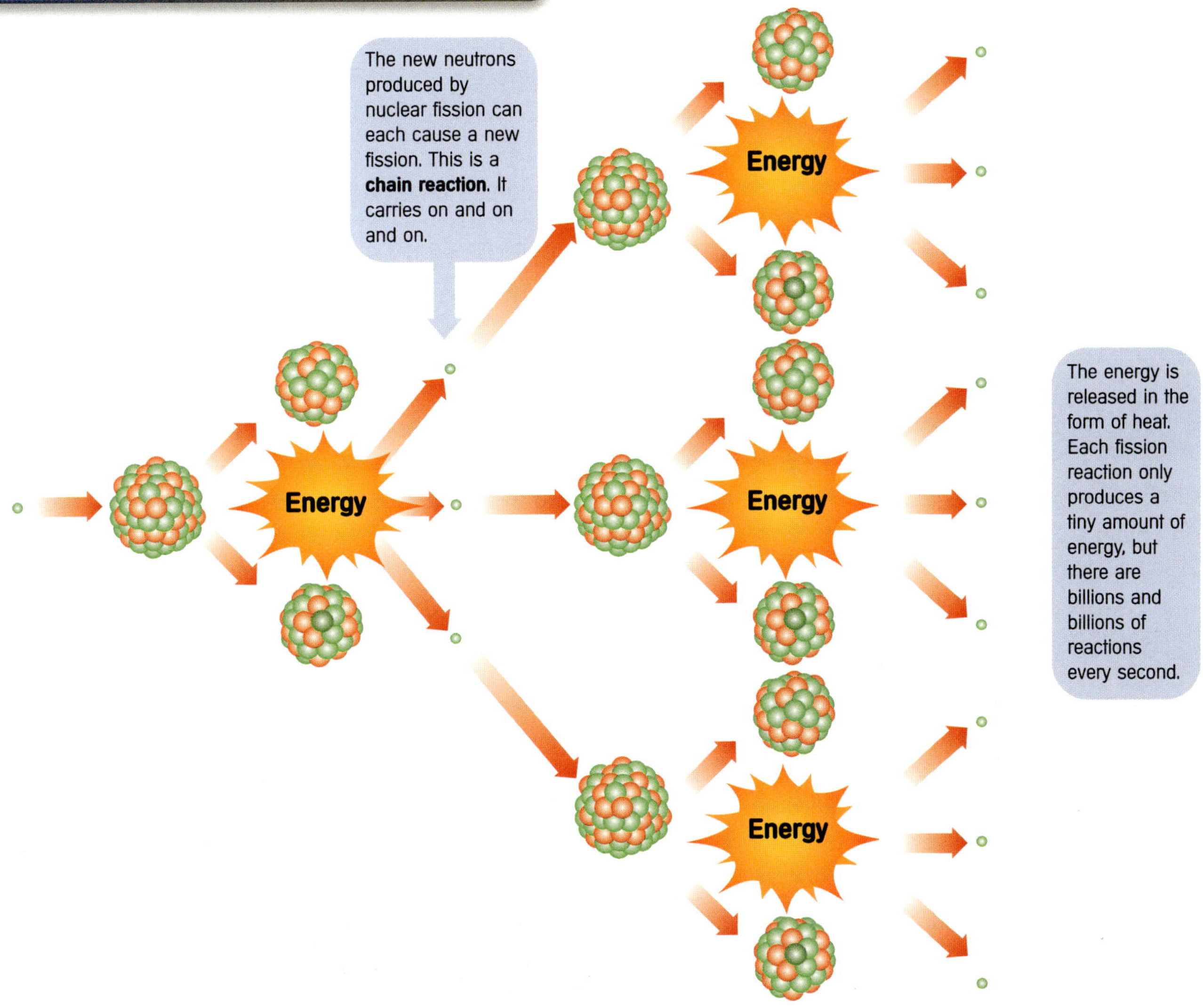

Physics Unit 2 Summary

Speed

Speed = how fast an object is moving.

Distance–time graphs represent the **speed** of an object.

Velocity = the **speed and direction** of an object.

$$\text{Speed (m/s)} = \frac{\text{Distance travelled (m)}}{\text{Time taken (s)}}$$

Acceleration

The **acceleration** or **deceleration** of an object is the rate at which its **velocity changes**.

Velocity–time graphs represent the **acceleration** of an object.

$$\text{Acceleration (m/s}^2\text{) (or deceleration)} = \frac{\text{Change in velocity (m/s)}}{\text{Time taken for change (s)}}$$

Forces

Forces = pushes or pulls that affect the movement of an object.

Resultant force = the sum of all the forces that act on an object.

Equal and **opposite** forces are **balanced**. Balanced forces keep the movement of an object **constant**.

Unequal and **opposite** forces are unbalanced. **Unbalanced** forces **change** the movement of an object.

Terminal velocity is a steady falling speed, i.e. gravity and air resistance are equal.

Stopping distance = thinking distance + braking distance. Stopping distance can be affected by speed, weather conditions and external factors affecting the driver or car.

Kinetic Energy

Kinetic energy = the energy an object has because of its **movement**. It depends on the **mass** and **speed** of the object.

HT

$$\text{Kinetic energy (J)} = \frac{1}{2} \times \text{Mass (kg)} \times \text{Speed}^2\ (\text{m/s})^2$$

Momentum = a measure of the state of motion of an object. It depends on the **mass** and **velocity** of the object. Momentum has both **magnitude** and **direction**.

In a **collision** or **explosion**, **momentum** is **conserved** providing no external forces act.

Physics Unit 2 Summary

Static Electricity

Static electricity is created when two insulating materials are rubbed against each other.

Material minus electrons = positively charged

Material plus electrons = negatively charged

Like charges **repel**. Different charges **attract**.

Static electricity can be discharged by connecting it to earth with a conductor. Can be used in smoke precipitators and photocopiers.

Circuits, Current and Power

The amount of electric current that flows through a component depends on...
- **potential difference** across component
- resistance of component.

Greater **potential difference** across a component = greater **current** through the component.

Direct current → flows in the same direction. **Alternating current** → constantly changes direction.

Circuit breakers and **fuses** are safety devices designed to **break** a circuit if the current becomes **too high**.

Electrical energy can be transformed into other types of energy. The **rate** of this transformation is the **power**.

HT

Charge (coulomb, C) = Current (amp, A) x Time (second, s)

Atoms

Atom = protons + neutrons + electrons. Atom has no overall charge.

Atomic number = number of protons. **Mass number** = number of protons and neutrons.

Radiation

Background radiation is not harmful.

Ions are **charged particles** caused by electrons being knocked out of atoms.

Alpha and **beta radiation** is **ionising** radiation.

Nuclear Fission and Fusion

Nuclear fusion = joining of atomic nuclei.

Nuclear fission = splitting of atomic nuclei.

Physics Practice Questions

1 This question is about speed. You may find this formula useful: $\textbf{Speed (m/s)} = \dfrac{\textbf{Distance travelled (m)}}{\textbf{Time taken (s)}}$

Match the letters A, B, C and D with the statements 1 to 4 below.

A 42 **B** 156.97

C 1.60 **D** 10.52

1 What is the speed, in m/s, of a runner who travels a distance of 100 metres in 9.5 seconds? ☐

2 A car travels a distance of 5023m at a speed of 32m/s. How many seconds does the car take to travel the distance? ☐

3 It takes 3 seconds for an arrow to hit a target. If the arrow travels at a speed of 14m/s, how many metres from the target is the archer standing? ☐

4 It takes a girl 19 minutes to walk to school and the school is 1827 metres away from her house. What is her walking speed, in m/s? ☐

2 This question is about forces.

a) In what unit are forces measured? ....

b) With what symbols are forces represented on diagrams? ....

c) If a car travels at a constant speed, are the forces acting on the car balanced or unbalanced?

....

3 This question is about components in a circuit.

a) Explain what would happen to the resistance if the temperature of a thermistor increases.

....

b) Sketch a diagram of a light dependent resistor.

4 Complete the table about the mass and charges of the parts of an atom.

Atomic Particle	Relative Mass	Relative Change
a)	1	+1
Neutron	**b)**	0
c)	0 (nearly)	**d)** ....

5 This question is about how a circuit breaker and a fuse work.

Match the letters A, B, C and D with the gaps 1 to 4 in the table.

A Circuit is broken

B Strength of electromagnet increases

C No current flows

D Current larger than current rating of fuse

Circuit Breaker	Fuse
Current becomes too high	**2** ....
1	Fuse wire melts
Pair of contacts are pulled apart	Circuit is broken
3	**4** ....
Appliance or user is protected	Appliance or user is protected

6 The graph below shows the velocity of a motorbike.

a) In terms of speed, describe how the motorbike is travelling at the following stages:

i) Stage A

....

ii) Stage C

....

iii) Stage E

....

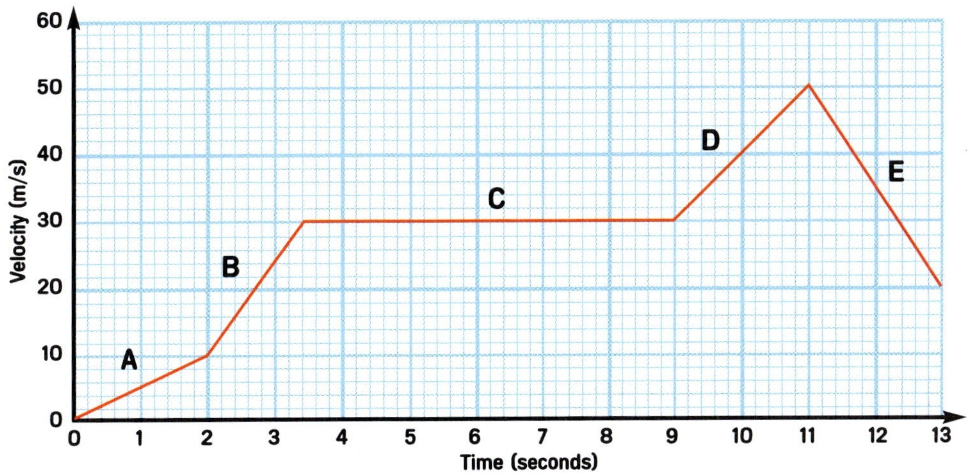

b) Calculate the acceleration at Stage D. Show your workings.

....

....

....

7 Calculate the momentum of a car that has a mass of 1700kg and is travelling at a velocity of 45m/s.

....

....

....

Glossary of Key Words

Acceleration – the rate at which an object increases in speed.

Acid – a compound that has a pH value lower than 7.

Activation energy – the minimum amount of energy required to cause a reaction.

Aerobic respiration – respiration which uses oxygen.

Alkali – a compound that has a pH value higher than 7.

Allele – an alternative form of a particular gene.

Alternating current (a.c.) – an electric current which changes direction of flow continuously.

Amylase – an enzyme that breaks down starch.

Atom economy – a measure of the amount of reactants in a chemical reaction which end up as useful products; usually expressed as a percentage.

Atomic number – the number of protons in an atom.

Attraction – the drawing together of two materials with different charges.

Bile – a greenish-yellow fluid produced by the liver.

Biomass – the mass of a plant or animal minus the water content.

Carbon cycle – the constant recycling of carbon by the processes in life, death and decay.

Catalyst – a substance that increases the rate of a chemical reaction without being changed itself.

Cell – a fundamental unit of a living organism.

Charged – having an overall positive or negative electrical charge.

Chlorophyll – the green pigment found in most plants, responsible for photosynthesis.

Chloroplast – tiny structure in the cytoplasm of plant cells which contain chlorophyll.

Chromosomes – long molecules found in the nucleus of all cells containing DNA.

Circuit breaker – a safety device which automatically breaks an electric circuit when it becomes overloaded.

Community – all the living organisms in an area or habitat.

Compound – a substance consisting of two or more elements chemically combined together.

Covalent bond – a bond between two atoms in which both atoms share one or more electrons.

Current – the rate of flow of an electrical charge, measured in amperes (A).

Cytoplasm – the substance found in living cells (outside the nucleus) where chemical reactions take place.

Decay – to rot or decompose.

Deceleration – the rate at which an object slows down.

Detritus – organic material formed from dead and decomposing plants and animals.

Diabetes – a condition in which a person's blood glucose level rises to very high concentrations.

Differentiate – to make / become different.

Diffusion – the moving of particles from high to low concentration.

Diode – an electrical device that allows current to flow in one direction.

Direct current (d.c.) – an electric current which flows in one direction.

Distance – the space between two points.

Distance–time graph – a graph showing distance travelled against time taken; the line represents speed.

DNA – nucleic acid which contains the genetic information carried by every cell.

Glossary of Key Words

Earthed – connecting the metal case of an electrical appliance to the earth pin of a plug.

Electrodes – pieces of metal or carbon which allow electric current to enter and leave during electrolysis.

Electrolysis – the process by which an electric current causes a solution to undergo chemical decomposition.

Electron – a negatively charged subatomic particle that orbits the nucleus.

Electrostatic – producing or caused by static electricity.

Endothermic – a reaction that takes in heat from its surroundings.

Energy – the capacity of a physical system to do work; measured in joules (J).

Environment – the conditions around an organism.

Enzyme – a protein catalyst which alters the rate of a particular biochemical reaction.

Exothermic – a reaction that gives out heat to its surroundings.

Fertilisation – the fusion of the male gamete with the female gamete.

Food chain – the feeding relationship between organisms.

Force – a push or pull acting on an object.

Frequency – the number of times something happens in 1 second; measured in hertz.

Friction – the resistive force between two surfaces as they move over each other.

Fuse – a thin piece of metal which overheats and melts to break an electric circuit if it's overloaded.

Gamete – a specialised sex cell formed by meiosis.

Gene – a small section of DNA of a chromosome which determines a particular characteristic.

Insoluble – a substance that will not dissolve in a solvent.

Insulin – a hormone which controls blood glucose concentration.

Ion (electrolyte) – a particle that has a positive or negative electrical charge.

Ionic bond – the process by which two or more atoms lose or gain electrons to become charged ions.

Isotopes – atoms of the same element which contain different numbers of neutrons.

Kinetic energy – the energy possessed by an object due to its movement.

Lipase – an enzyme which breaks down fat into fatty acids and glycerol.

Mass – the quantity of matter in an object.

Mass number – the total number of protons and neutrons present in an atom.

Microorganism – a very small organism.

Mineral ions – charged particles formed from elements (or groups of elements) which plants need for healthy growth.

Mitochondria – the structure in the cytoplasm where energy is produced from chemical reactions.

Mitosis – cell division that forms two daughter cells, each with the same number of chromosomes as the parent cell.

Mole (mol) – the molar mass of a substance, i.e. the mass in grams of 6×10^{23} particles.

Momentum – a measure of the state of motion of an object as a product of its mass and velocity.

Nanoscience – dealing with materials that have a very small grain size, in the order of 1–100nm.

Neutralisation – a reaction between an acid and a base which forms a neutral solution.

Neutron – a subatomic particle found in the nucleus which has no charge.

Newton – a measure of force.

Nitrate – any compound containing the nitrate radical (NO_3).

Nuclear fission – the splitting of atomic nuclei.

Nuclear fusion – the joining together of atomic nuclei.

Nucleus (Biology) – the control centre of a cell.

Nucleus – the small central core of an atom, consisting of protons and neutrons.

Osmosis – the movement of water from a dilute to a more concentrated solution across a semi-permeable membrane.

Oxidation – a reaction involving the gain of oxygen, the loss of hydrogen, or the loss of electrons.

Parallel circuit – a circuit where there are two (or more) paths for the current to take.

pH – a measure of acidity or alkalinity.

Photosynthesis – the chemical process that uses light energy to produce glucose in plants.

Potential difference/voltage – the difference in electrical charge between two charged points.

Precipitation – the removal of particles from a solution.

Protease – an enzyme used to break down proteins into amino acids.

Proton – a positively charged subatomic particle found in the nucleus.

Radiation – electromagnetic particles / rays emitted by a radioactive substance.

Reduction – a reaction involving the loss of oxygen, the gain of hydrogen, or the gain of electrons.

Relative formula mass (M_r) – the sum of the atomic masses of all atoms in a molecule.

Repulsion – the pushing away of two materials with the same charge.

Resistance – opposition to the flow of an electric current.

Resistor – an electrical device that resists the flow of an electric current.

Respiration – the process of converting glucose into energy inside cells.

Resultant force – the combined effect of all the forces acting on an object.

Reversible reaction – a reaction in which products can react to reform the original reactants.

Ribosomes – small structures found in the cytoplasm of living cells, where protein synthesis takes place.

Salt – the product of a chemical reaction between a base and an acid.

Series circuit – a circuit where there is one path for the current to take.

Smart materials – materials which have one or more properties that can be altered.

Specialised – developed for a special function.

Speed – the rate at which an object moves.

Static electricity – electricity produced by friction.

Stem cell – a cell of human embryos or adult bone marrow which has yet to differentiate.

Terminal velocity – the constant maximum velocity reached by a falling object (i.e. gravitational force is equal to the frictional forces).

Thermistor – a resistor whose resistance varies with temperature.

Thermoregulation – maintenance of a constant body temperature in warm-blooded animals.

Transfer – to move energy from one place to another.

Transform – to change energy from one form into another, e.g. electrical energy to heat energy.

Urea – toxins produced when proteins are broken down.

Vacuole – a fluid-filled sac found in cytoplasm.

Velocity – the speed at which an object moves in a particular direction.

Velocity–time graph – a graph showing velocity against time taken; the line represents acceleration.

Weight – the gravitational force exerted on an object.

Work – the energy transfer that occurs when a force causes a body to move a certain distance.

Zygote – a cell formed by the fusion of the nuclei of a male sex cell and a female sex cell (gametes).

HT **Equilibrium** – the state in which a chemical reaction proceeds at the same rate as its reverse reaction (the reactants are balanced).

Meiosis – cell division that forms daughter cells with half the number of chromosomes of the parent cell.

Relative atomic mass (A_r) – the average mass of an atom of an element compared with twelfth of a carbon atom.

Yield – the amount of a product obtained from a reaction.

Answers to Practice Questions

Biology

1. **a)** A = cell membrane; B = nucleus; C = ribosome.
   b) This is where most energy is released during respiration.
   c) Cell membrane.
2. **a)** light; carbon dioxide; water; chlorophyll.
   b) glucose; oxygen.
   c) **i)** Diffusion
   ii) Osmosis
   d) Yellow leaves.
3. A = blackbirds; B = ladybirds; C = greenfly; D = oak tree.
4. **a)** ii) The pancreas ✔
   b) iii) It could rise to a fatally high level ✔
5. **a)** **Accept any two:** respiration, protein synthesis, photosynthesis.
   b) temperature; pH.
   c) Bile neutralises stomach acid and emulsifies fats.
6. **a)** iii) DNA ✔
   b) ii) 23 ✔
   c) iv) 100% ✔

Chemistry

1. **a)** i) Electron ✔
   b) iv) 12 ✔
   c) i) Group 1 ✔
   d) i) Positive ✔
2. **a)** The reaction is reversible.
   b) It means that heat (energy) is given out.
   c) **Nitrogen:** from the air (atmosphere); **Hydrogen:** from natural gas.
   d) There are more moles of reactants than products, i.e. 4 molecules of reactants are changed into 2 molecules of product.
   e) **i)** Iron
   ii) To speed up the reaction.
3. **a)** Relative formula mass = 23 + 16 +1 = 40.
   b) 16 / 40 x 100 = 40%.
   c) 40 / 100 x 5 = 2g.
   d) 1 mole of NaOH = 23 + 16 + 1 = 40g.
   4 moles of NaOH = 40 x 4 = **160g**.
4. **a)** Each carbon atom forms four strong covalent bonds with other carbon atoms.
   b) Very high melting points.
5. **a)** Chlorine
   b) The ions are positively charged and they are attracted to the negative (oppositely charged) electrode.
   c) Reduction is the gain of electrons and oxidation is the loss of electrons.
6. **a)** Potassium chloride
   b) Sulfuric acid
   c) Sodium hydroxide
   d) Barium sulfate + zinc chloride
   e) Barium sulfate

Answers to Practice Questions

Physics

1. **1** D, **2** B, **3** A, **4** C.
2. **a)** Newtons
   b) Arrows
   c) Balanced
3. **a)** The resistance would decrease.
   b) 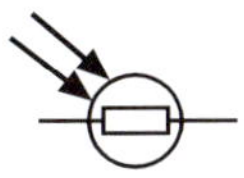
4. **a)** Proton
   b) 1
   c) Electron
   d) -1
5. **1** B, **2** D, **3** A, **4** C.
6. **a)** **i)** Speeding up / accelerating.
   ii) Steady or constant speed.
   iii) Slowing down / decelerating.
   b) Acceleration $= \frac{\text{Change in velocity}}{\text{Time taken}} = \frac{20\text{m/s}}{2\text{s}}$
   $= 10\text{m/s}^2$.
7. Momentum = Mass x Velocity = 1700 x 45 = 76 500kg m/s

Notes

Acknowledgements

Acknowledgements

The authors and publisher would like to thank everyone who has contributed to this book:

p.10 ©iStockphoto.com / Peter Galbraith
p.20 ©iStockphoto.com / Helle Bro Clemmensen

ISBN 978-1-905896-20-2

Published by Lonsdale, a division of Huveaux Plc.

Authors: Andrew Catterall
Lynn Henfield
Christine Horbury

Project Editor: Charlotte Christensen

Cover Design: Angela English

Concept Design: Sarah Duxbury and Helen Jacobs

Designer: Ian Wrigley

Artwork: Lonsdale and HL Studios

Author Information

Andrew Catterall (Physics), Lynn Henfield (Biology) and Christine Horbury (Chemistry) are all science consultants for LEAs. They work closely with the exam boards and have an excellent understanding of the new science specifications, which they are helping to implement in local schools.

As former science teachers, with over 70 years' experience between them, their main objective in writing this book was to produce a user-friendly revision guide for students, which would also act as a useful reference for teachers. As such, this guide provides full coverage of all the essential material, cross-referenced to the specification for ease of use and presented in a clear and interesting manner that is accessible to everyone.

Index

Periodic Table

Key

relative atomic mass **atomic symbol** name atomic (proton) number

1	2											3	4	5	6	7	0
						1 **H** hydrogen 1											4 **He** helium 2
7 **Li** lithium 3	9 **Be** beryllium 4											11 **B** boron 5	12 **C** carbon 6	14 **N** nitrogen 7	16 **O** oxygen 8	19 **F** fluorine 9	20 **Ne** neon 10
23 **Na** sodium 11	24 **Mg** magnesium 12											27 **Al** aluminium 13	28 **Si** silicon 14	31 **P** phosphorus 15	32 **S** sulfur 16	35.5 **Cl** chlorine 17	40 **Ar** argon 18
39 **K** potassium 19	40 **Ca** calcium 20	45 **Sc** scandium 21	48 **Ti** titanium 22	51 **V** vanadium 23	52 **Cr** chromium 24	55 **Mn** manganese 25	56 **Fe** iron 26	59 **Co** cobalt 27	59 **Ni** nickel 28	63.5 **Cu** copper 29	65 **Zn** zinc 30	70 **Ga** gallium 31	73 **Ge** germanium 32	75 **As** arsenic 33	79 **Se** selenium 34	80 **Br** bromine 35	84 **Kr** krypton 36
85 **Rb** rubidium 37	88 **Sr** strontium 38	89 **Y** yttrium 39	91 **Zr** zirconium 40	93 **Nb** niobium 41	96 **Mo** molybdenum 42	[98] **Tc** technetium 43	101 **Ru** ruthenium 44	103 **Rh** rhodium 45	106 **Pd** palladium 46	108 **Ag** silver 47	112 **Cd** cadmium 48	115 **In** indium 49	119 **Sn** tin 50	122 **Sb** antimony 51	128 **Te** tellurium 52	127 **I** iodine 53	131 **Xe** xenon 54
133 **Cs** caesium 55	137 **Ba** barium 56	139 **La*** lanthanum 57	178 **Hf** hafnium 72	181 **Ta** tantalum 73	184 **W** tungsten 74	186 **Re** rhenium 75	190 **Os** osmium 76	192 **Ir** iridium 77	195 **Pt** platinum 78	197 **Au** gold 79	201 **Hg** mercury 80	204 **Tl** thallium 81	207 **Pb** lead 82	209 **Bi** bismuth 83	[209] **Po** polonium 84	[210] **At** astatine 85	[222] **Rn** radon 86
[223] **Fr** francium 87	[226] **Ra** radium 88	[227] **Ac*** actinium 89	[261] **Rf** rutherfordium 104	[262] **Db** dubnium 105	[266] **Sg** seaborgium 106	[264] **Bh** bohrium 107	[277] **Hs** hassium 108	[268] **Mt** meitnerium 109	[271] **Ds** darmstadtium 110	[272] **Rg** roentgenium 111							

Elements which have atomic numbers 112–116 have been reported but not fully authenticated.

*The Lanthanides (atomic numbers 58–71) and the Actinides (atomic numbers 90–103) have been omitted.

Cu and Cl have not been rounded to the nearest whole number.

→ The lines of elements going across are called **periods**.

↓ The columns of elements going down are called **groups**.